Where the BUFFALO Roam

2003

CASPER, WYOMING

A BENEFIT FOR
THE NICOLAYSEN ART MUSEUM & DISCOVERY CENTER

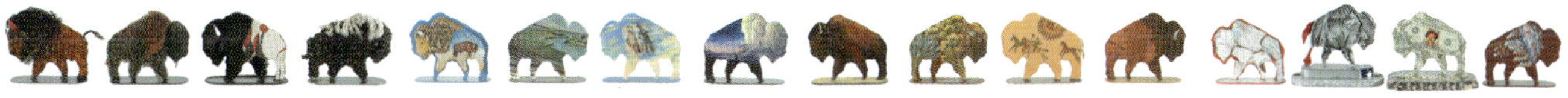

Holly P. Turner, Editor

ISBN# 0-9714725-9-9 Softcover
Library of Congress Control Number : 2003107676

This book was printed in the United States of America

All Photography (unless otherwise noted) by
Bruce Nichols, Mountain Sun Photo, Casper, Wyoming

Book Design: Antelope Design
Published by Pronghorn Press

www.pronghornpress.org

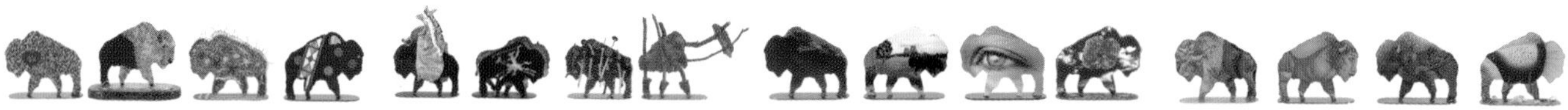

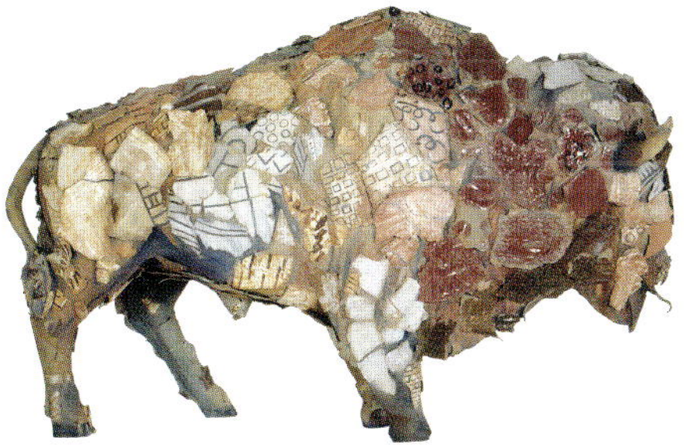

TABLE OF CONTENTS

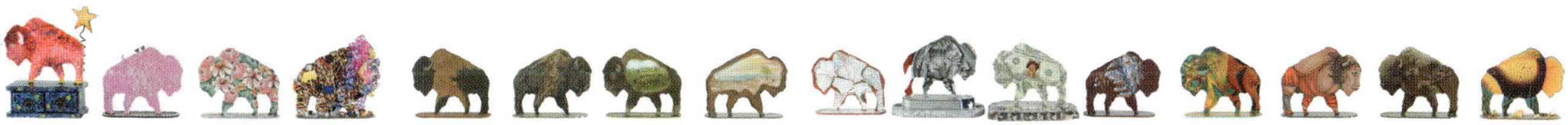

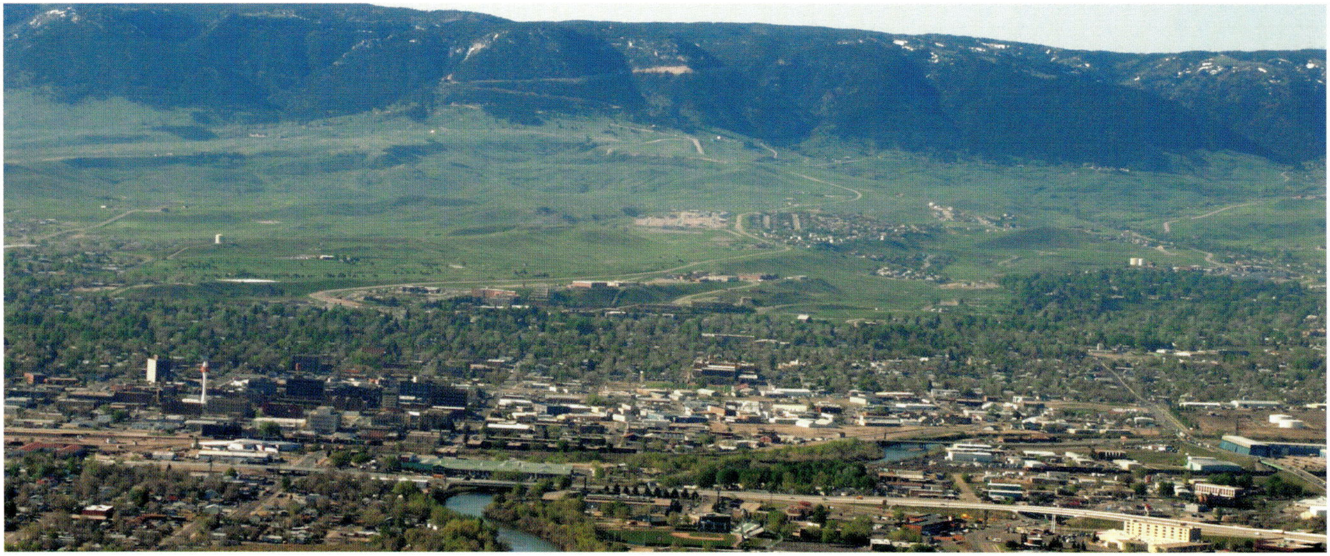

DEAR FRIENDS,

It is my pleasure to welcome you to ***Where the Buffalo Roam 2003***, an outstanding project and great source of pride for our community.

Throughout the summer ***Where the Buffalo Roam*** will be displayed in various locations around the community, with thirty buffalo, all painted and decorated by talented regional artists. Please join me in experiencing this exhibit and learning the history of our community and surrounding area.

The Buffalo will become a source of community pride. It is one more great reason for Casperites and visitors to spend time in our city.

Once again, welcome! Enjoy this public art exhibition.

Sincerely,

Barbara A. Peryam
Mayor

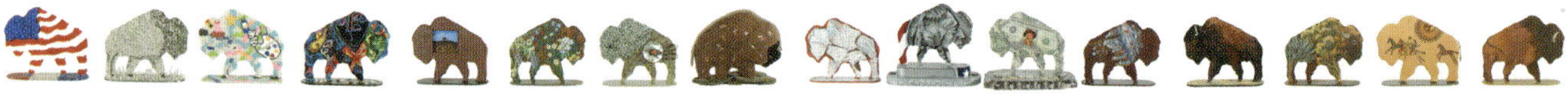

DEAR BUFFALO LOVERS!!

Welcome to ***Where the Buffalo Roam 2003*** in Casper, Wyoming. It is with great pleasure that we present these spectacular creations by thirty artists who participated in this exciting and memorable event. Some of these are the works of known and revered artists and others the labors of aspiring and young artists, created for exhibition at a variety of sponsor locations and for public interaction and enjoyment.

Why Buffalo? We imagined a time when these regal animals roamed freely in our state. Daily we see the Buffalo on our state flag, and we think of their courage and strength. They represent hope for us today and for the future. The excitement and enthusiasm for this project has been witnessed in the smiles they bring to both children and adults who are touched by the creative and whimsical herd. These thirty Buffalo beauties have quickly become beloved by the community. We are so thankful to the countless people who have made this project possible.

A special thanks to our artists for their unique, creative and amazing vision and to our generous sponsors who made it possible for the Buffalo to come to life. We also extend thanks to our business community, city leaders, visionary board, volunteer committees and incredible staff. Without their countless hours this event would not be possible. Every one of you has inspired and renewed us and it is our sincere hope that you enjoy this commemorative book as much as we have enjoyed presenting ***Where the Buffalo Roam.***

This event will make it possible for the Nicolaysen Art Museum and Discovery Center to continue excellent exhibitions, children's educational programs, and to increase our endowment for the citizens and guests of Wyoming.

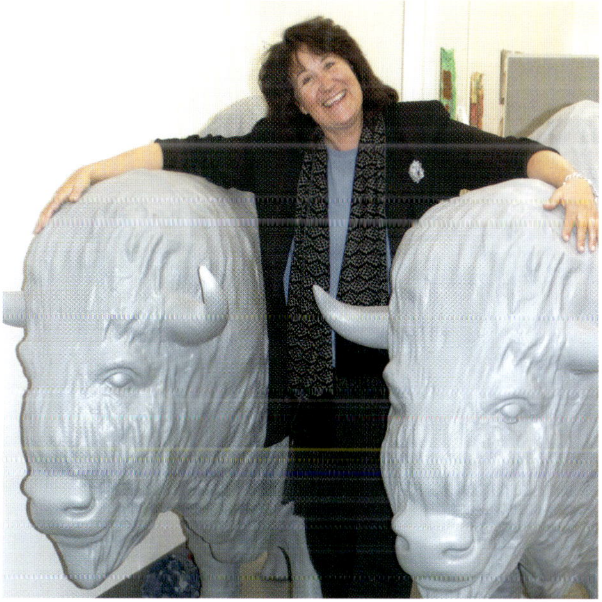

Holly Turner
Executive Director

Gary Berchenbriter
Board of Directors
President

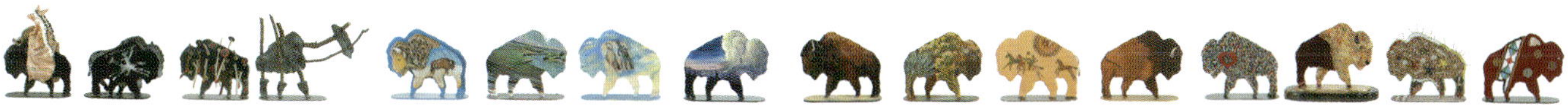

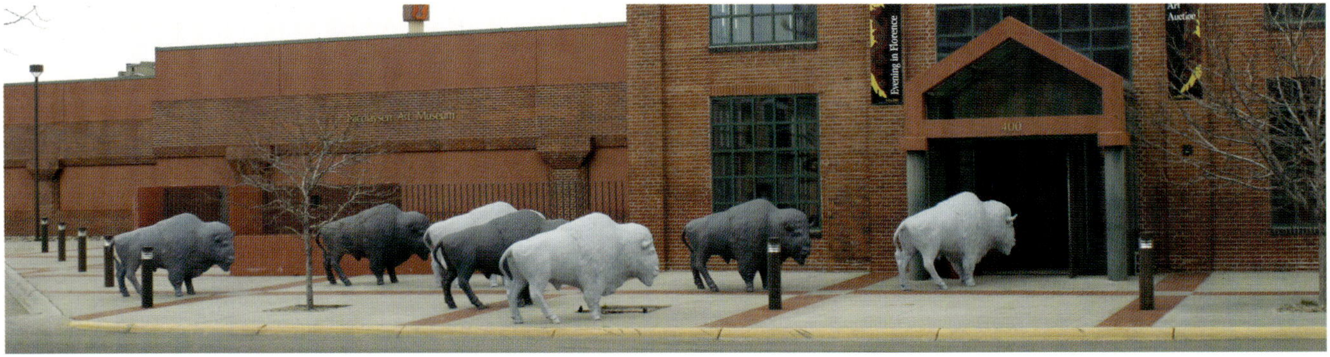

THE NICOLAYSEN ART MUSEUM & DISCOVERY CENTER: A HISTORY

The Nicolaysen Art Museum and Discovery Center has occupied its current location at 400 East Collins since 1990, when the extensive renovation of the building was completed. There are many people who remember the site as the Casper Lumber Company Building and others who remember when it was an electricity generating plant.

Photo: Courtesy of the NIC

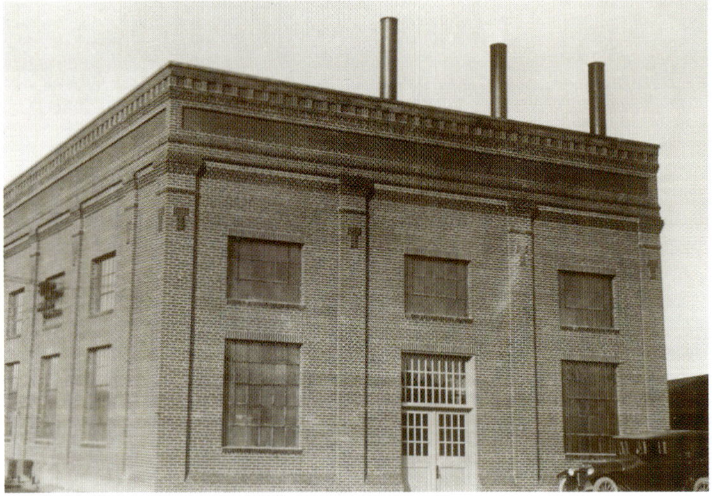

THE BUILDING

The original generating plant owned by the Casper Electric Company opened on September 23, 1908, about four blocks west at the corner of Collins and Center streets. The original building at 400 E. Collins Drive was the Wyoming Electric Company, which began operating on October 6, 1913. After a devastating fire at the Casper Electric Company on January 4, 1918 the two companies merged to form the Natrona County Electric Company. In 1924 a new generating plant was built on this site when

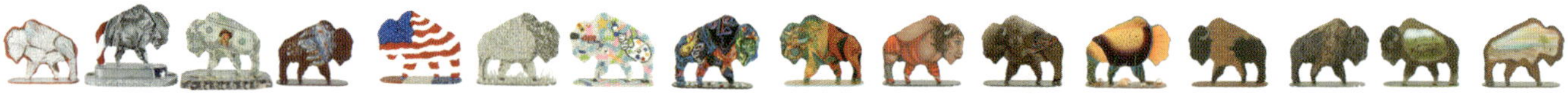

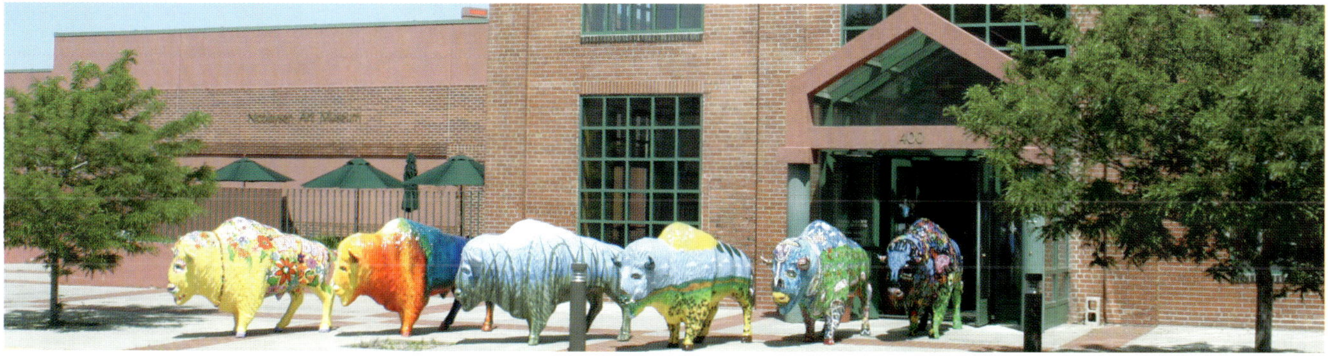

the Mountain States Power Company took over the building. The new plant had fourteen-inch thick walls and thirty-foot high ceilings. Power generation ended in 1950 when Mountain States Power merged with Pacific Power and Light. It was at this time that Casper Lumber moved in and sold lumber and hardware to Casper residents until 1976. The vacant building became a target for projectiles and graffiti. It stood as a slowly crumbling landmark for twelve years until it was purchased in 1988 as the permanent home for the Nicolaysen Art Museum and Discovery Center. In August of 1988 research done by High Country Historians concluded that the building was eligible for nomination to the National Register of Historical Places. However, there is no evidence that such nomination took place.

The November/December 1990 issue of *Historic Preservation* ran an article about the New NIC building by author Laura C. Smith titled "Artistic Outpost: A first-class museum reenergizes a power plant in Casper, Wyoming". The article gives a history of the building and describes the condition in which it stood before it was slated for renovation. The Gorder/South Group of Casper undertook the task of keeping the historical integrity of the building and making the structure safe, bringing utilities up to code, and a landmark of which the city could be proud. Construction and renovation began in February of 1989, lasted 330 days and cost 2.6 million dollars to complete. The building was gutted, leaving only the brick walls. The original brick part of the building became the lobby, the offices and the Discovery Center. Two additions on the east and west created the galleries, the prep room, the collections vault, the loading dock, the kitchen, the coat hall, the bathrooms, and the shop for a total of 30,000 square feet. At the time the NIC was one of the newest and most impressive climate controlled museums in the region.

The Discovery Center was the first art museum facility to offer hands-on participation and provide a permanent place within a museum for visitors of all ages to make art. The center was designed to be educational, flexible and fun. A place where children and adults can come and experiment with, learn about, and create art.

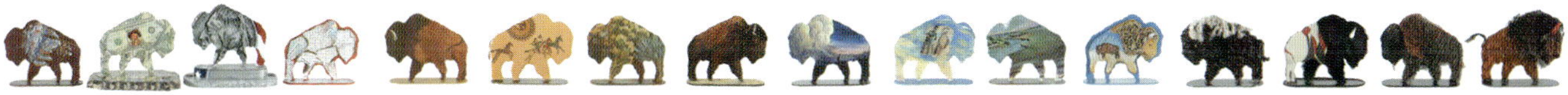

THE MUSEUM

The NIC's history begins in 1967 when Mary Durham and some friends opened the first Art show in the little white house that still stands at the corner of "A" and Park Streets. Contributors to "Gallery A", as it was called, supported the Museum enough that soon they needed a larger space to house all of their interests. In 1972, the newly renamed Central Wyoming Art Museum found the room it needed in a former furniture store on Rancho Road. The 7,000 square foot building provided more exhibit space as well as space for classes and other programs. However, meeting the mortgage payments became a struggle and in 1977 through the generosity of Gerald G. Nicolaysen the debt was paid off and the Board of Trustees re-christened the Museum in his honor. To that date the Museum had operated solely on a volunteer basis and as the Museum began to generate more interest and grow, it became clear that professional management was necessary. Dr. J. M. Neil became the Director in 1983 and Mary Lou Morrison, an artist and educator, became the director of the Children's Center, which is now known as the Discovery Center, when it opened in 1985.

The NIC's growth was substantial throughout the 1980s under the guidance of the Board and its Director. Visitation grew from 9,887 to 22,697 between 1983 and 1987 and steadily increased thereafter. A permanent collection was established and instead of renting all of its exhibits, the NIC began to tour many of its own. This expansion of interest in the museum led to an agreement between the Museum's Board of Trustees and the One-Cent Sales Tax Committee of Natrona County that a question of public support for a new facility for the NIC be put before the voters in November of 1984. It was by the vote of the electorate that funds were set aside for the purchase of land and the construction of a building. The Museum in turn had to raise an endowment large enough to maintain the facility without the use of further tax support.

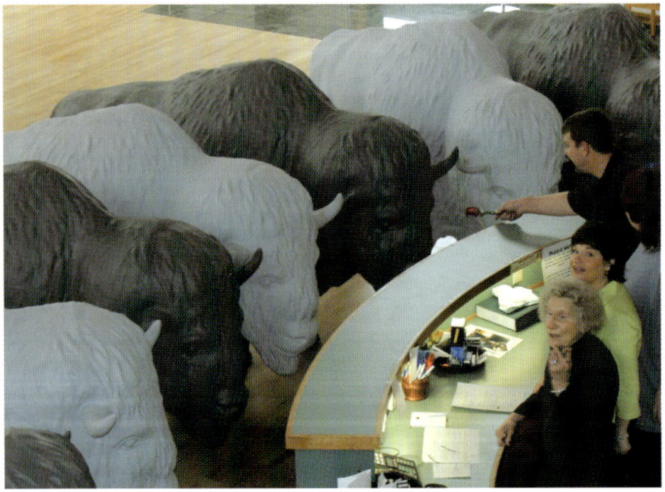

The Museum had a staff of eight; including Director, Discovery Center Coordinator, Registrar, Office Manager, Office Assistant/ Volunteer Coordinator, Building Engineer/ Custodian, and two Buyer/Managers for the gift shop. The new facility opened April 8, 1990.

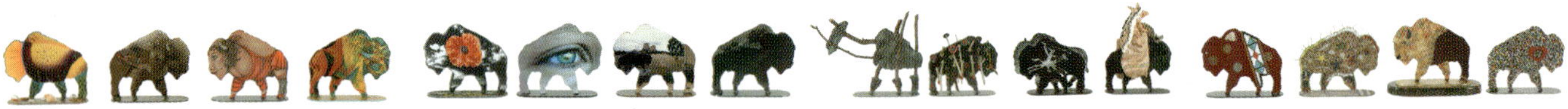

A CONDENSED HISTORY

For years the NIC has been the venue for many fine exhibits. The Museum has hosted exhibitions in all media: animated dinosaurs, color and black and white photography, paintings in oil, watercolor, pastel, gauche, on everything from parchment to steel. Sculptures, installations, and ceramics have been featured in many of the exhibits. The NIC has endeavored to stimulate discussion and thought through its exhibitions and educational programs.

TODAY

The NIC is still one of the largest and most impressive museums in the region, with over 37,000 visitors per year. The Discovery Center is still one of the largest hands-on art making facilities in the region. The NIC houses a permanent collection that includes local, regional, national and international artists. The NIC exhibits contemporary art from well-known local, regional and national artists. The museum shop has become an outlet for unique art related materials, a place to find that special gift, and a place to find unusual educational materials. The facilities are also used for receptions, weddings, meetings, parties, and gatherings of all sorts. The NIC has grown into a landmark museum for Casper, Wyoming and the region.

THE FUTURE

The Board of Directors and Staff have envisioned a Regional Contemporary Art Museum that not only continues to promote, educate and provoke thought, it also presents to the public a perspective that is unique and contemporary. The many volunteers who give so much to the museum are an essential part of the NIC's bright future. Plans are in the works for a NIC sponsored series of works by contemporary artists that would reflect and investigate the region in new and exciting ways. The NIC has refocused on its mission, which is "that the people of the Casper area appreciate and participate in the visual art". The NIC will accomplish its mission by providing; (1) extensive exhibition resources in the community, exposure to and education about diverse art forms and styles, and an emphasis on works produced in or associated with the Rocky Mountain West, (2) participation in the visual arts, (3) promoting the value of the arts, (4) assisting and supporting cooperation among community organizations in the Casper area. The years have been eventful, exciting and enlightening, but the next 5, 10, 15, will embody the purpose that originally set the Nicolaysen Art Museum and Discovery Center into motion.

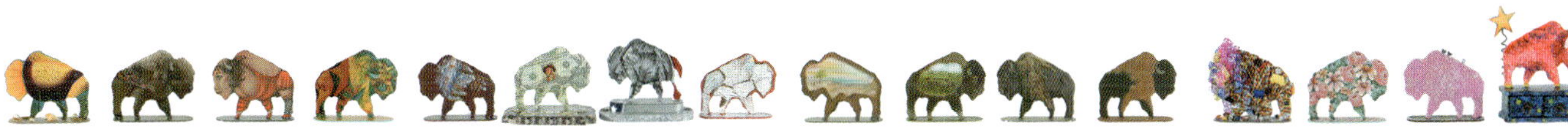

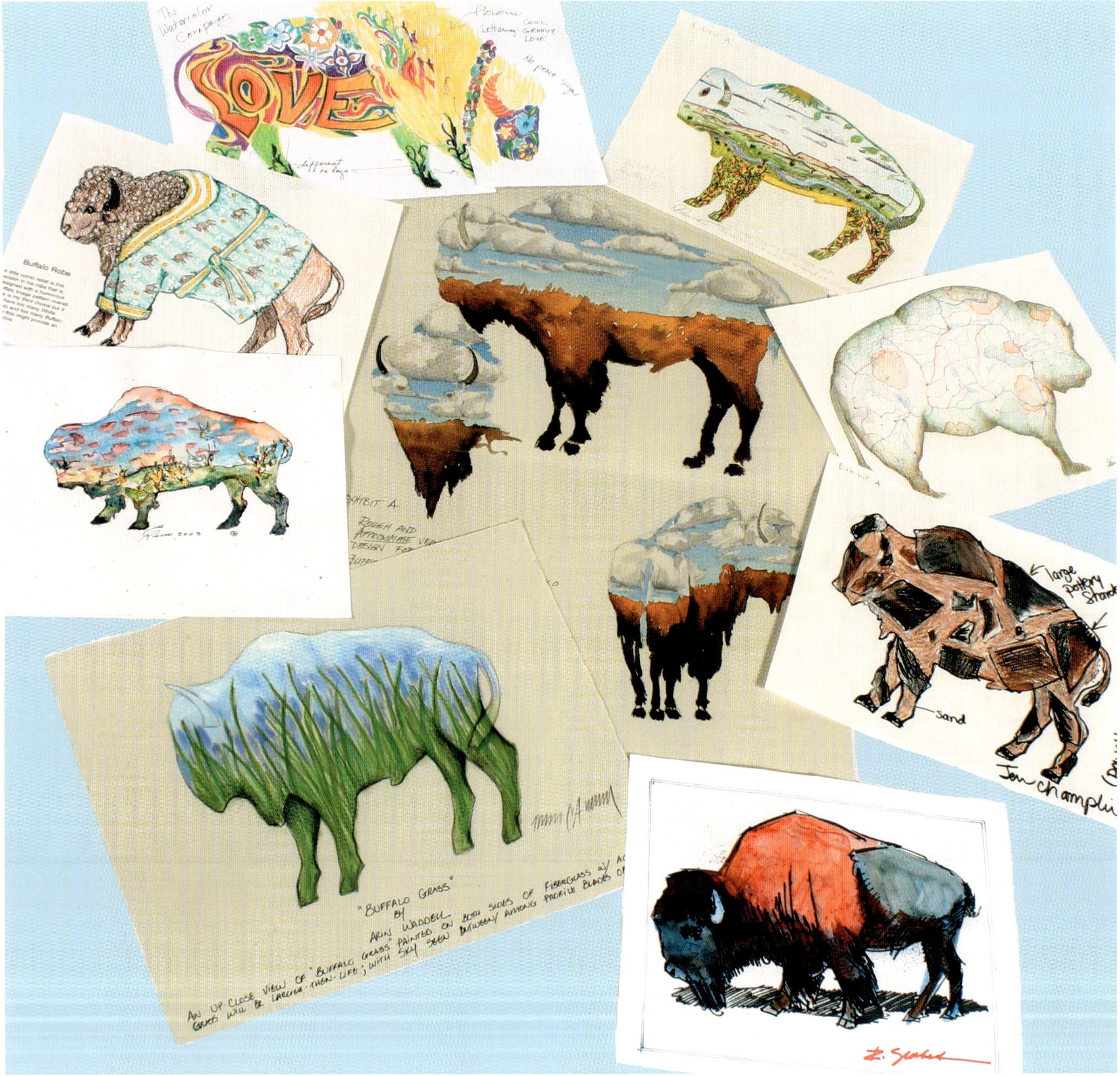
The Watercolor Company
Flowers
Lettering: COOL GROOVY LOVE
No peace signs
LOVE
Buffalo Robe
EXHIBIT A
ROUGH AND APPROXIMATE
DESIGN FOR
Exhibit A
large pottery Shards
Sand
"BUFFALO GRASS"
BY
ARIN WADDELL
AN UP CLOSE VIEW OF "BUFFALO GRASS" PAINTED ON BOTH SIDES OF FIBERGLASS W/
GRASS WILL BE LARGER-THAN-LIFE; WITH SKY SEEN BETWEEN/ AMONG PROFILE BLADES

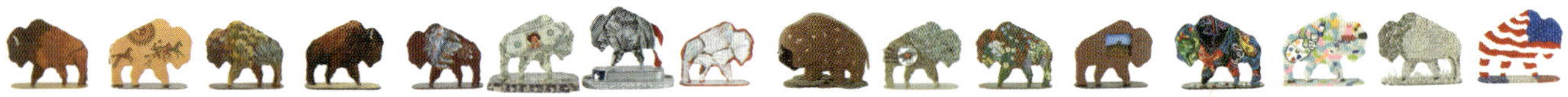

THE PROJECT

During the summer of 2002 we were reading and hearing much about other cities and their animal art parades. It was brought into focus during a summer trip to Billings, Montana where we enjoyed seeing their *Horse of Course* project. We consulted with their organizers and knew immediately that we could launch a wonderful and exciting parade right here in Casper as a way to merge art and commerce, stimulate community pride and raise funds for the Nicolaysen Art Museum.

We chose Buffalo. Why? Buffalo are an authentic and long time symbol of our American West. They were monarchs of the Great Plains and the Buffalo holds the place of honor in the center of Wyoming's state flag. In addition, we are in a small way, beginning to see them roaming our plains today.

We called the company (Fiberstock) who created the Billings horses. Lloyd Christensen, president, told us that although they had never worked with a Buffalo form, it so happened they had been thinking of creating one since they were, after all, located in Buffalo, Minnesota. This seemed to be fate, indeed. The NIC Board of Directors and staff quickly assented to this exciting venture. Thirty Buffalo were promptly ordered and our project found the title, ***Where the Buffalo Roam.***

Our initial contacts with artists, explaining our project and asking if they were interested in decorating a 100-pound life-size Buffalo, were enthusiastically received. Responses were many and varied. We heard,

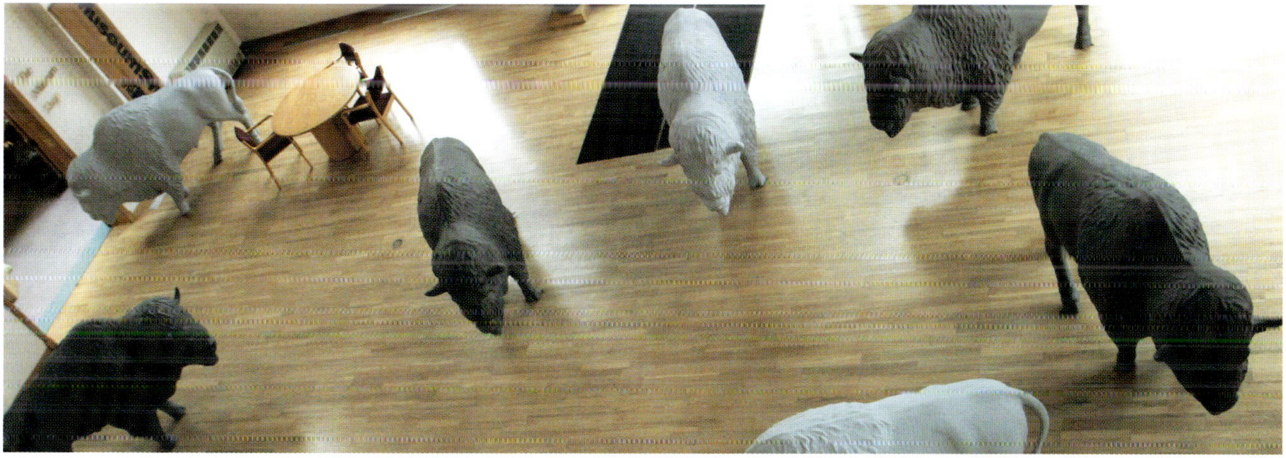

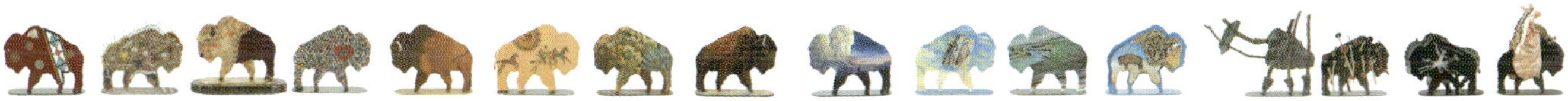

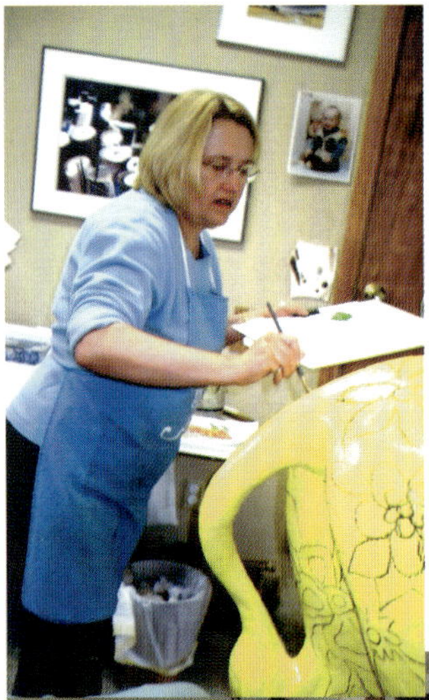

"Awesome!", "You're kidding", "It's about time someone did the Buffalo!", and included the question, "Can there be a team of artists on a single Buffalo?" The Artists' Committee spent long hours reviewing, gathering recommendations and researching artists before making their decisions. Finally the artists were chosen based on regional reputation and their submitted designs and sketches.

When the thirty life-size fiberglass "Buffalo in the buff" arrived at the NIC in February, 2003, a new challenge presented itself. They had to be transported to the artists, many of whom lived a considerable distance from Casper in places like Powell, in the northwestern corner of Wyoming, and Denver, Colorado, some 300 miles south. They were delivered to the artists by horse trailers, trucks, minivans and flatbeds, braving all kinds of weather — snow, wind, rain and hail. The artists received their honorarium along with their Buffalo and their work began.

Photo: Deb Penk

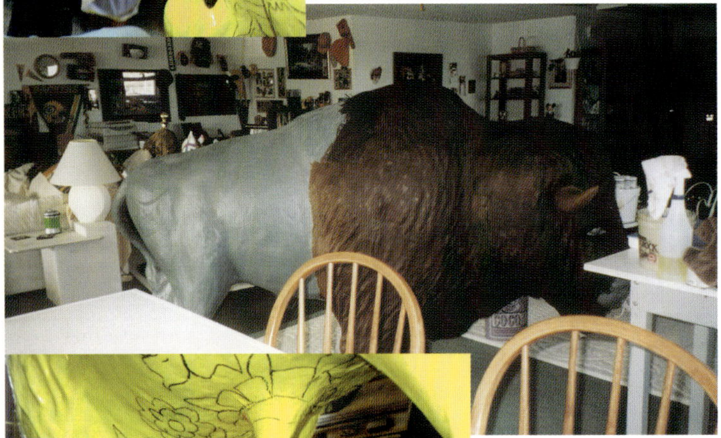

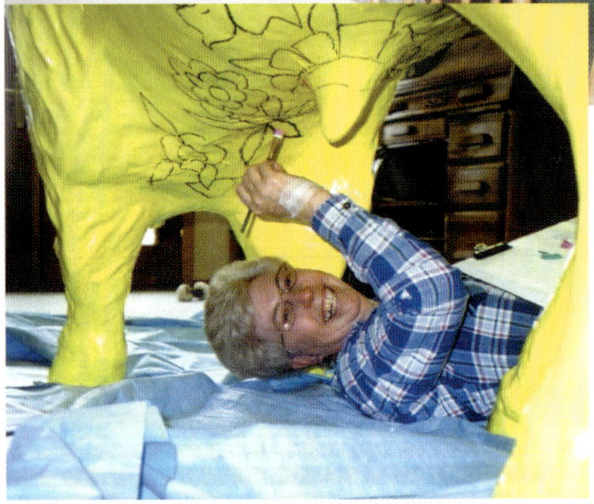

While the artists worked, excitement and momentum built here at the NIC. Not sure if the project would be well received or whether people would think it was crazy, we contacted potential businesses and individuals for sponsorships. Everyone did, indeed, think it was crazy, yet absolutely loved the concept. Curiosity was sparked by this new and different idea for Casper. Sponsors were on board quickly and in early May the finished Buffalo began to return to the NIC. They were fantastic; they were unique, and we were astounded. These symbols of strength, branded with the artists' designs, exceeded our expectations. As each Buffalo arrived, we heard a different artist story. They had lived with their animal, in their kitchens, in their living rooms, as well as in their studios. Over the time it took to decorate them, they became attached to their Buffalo and told us it was hard to let them go. Their neighbors, family and

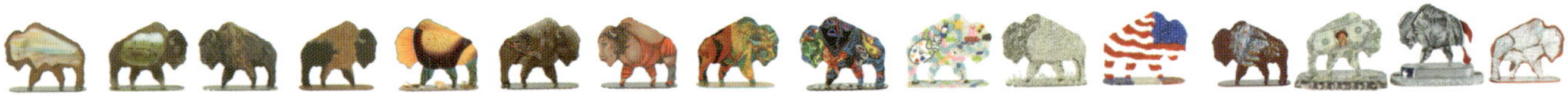

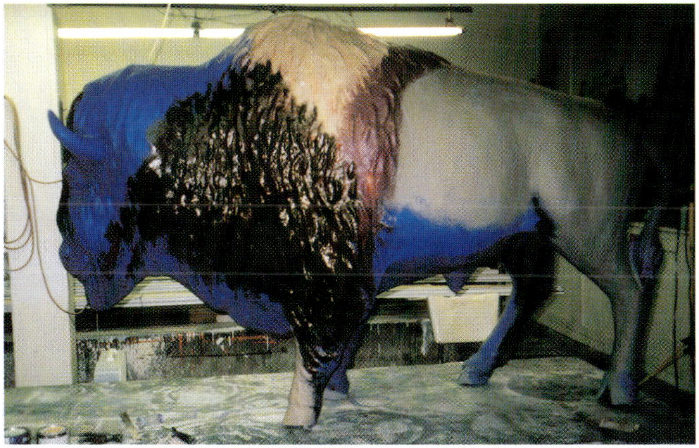

Photo: Robert Seabeck

friends had watched, made suggestions and admired the transformation, from grey to great.

In June, Casper started to have occasional "Buffalo sightings" as the animals arrived by truck and the Buffalo buzz accelerated noticeably. Meanwhile, the "Tech Committee" was busy working with the city of Casper and their zoning and transportation departments, lining up permits. The Committee also met with sign engineers to determine an appropriate size cement base that could withstand Wyoming's wind and weather. Wyoming Concrete Products donated the concrete, the city of Casper placed the cement pads and Merback Awards provided all plaques. Coliseum Motors clear-coated each Buffalo with an automobile clear coat for protection from the elements.

The thirty artful, aesthetic Buffalo were unveiled for the first time at an Artist/Sponsor Barbeque Reception in May. It was an amazing sight to see all the Buffalo together in the main gallery of the NIC and the overwhelming response of those viewing the Buffalo for the first time. Within a few days, the Casper Chamber of Commerce held a "Business Before Hours" breakfast meeting at the museum. There the Chamber members saw the Buffalo together for the last time prior to their public debut.

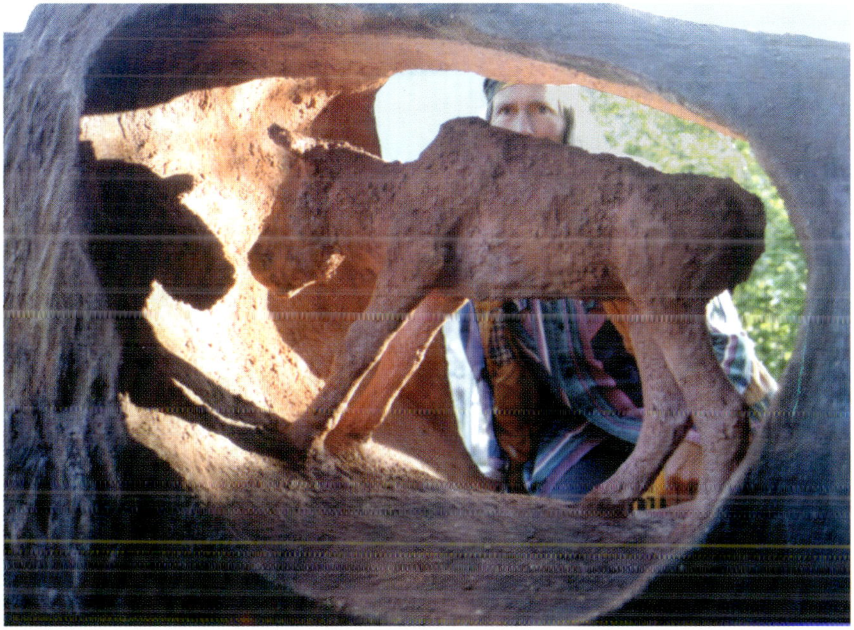

Photo: Elijah Cobb

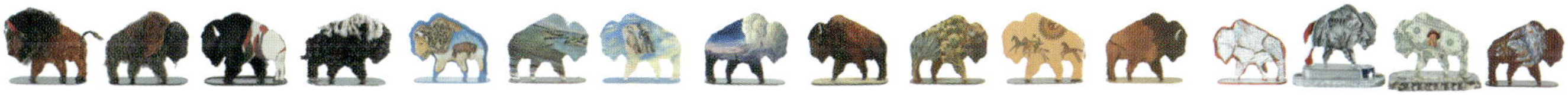

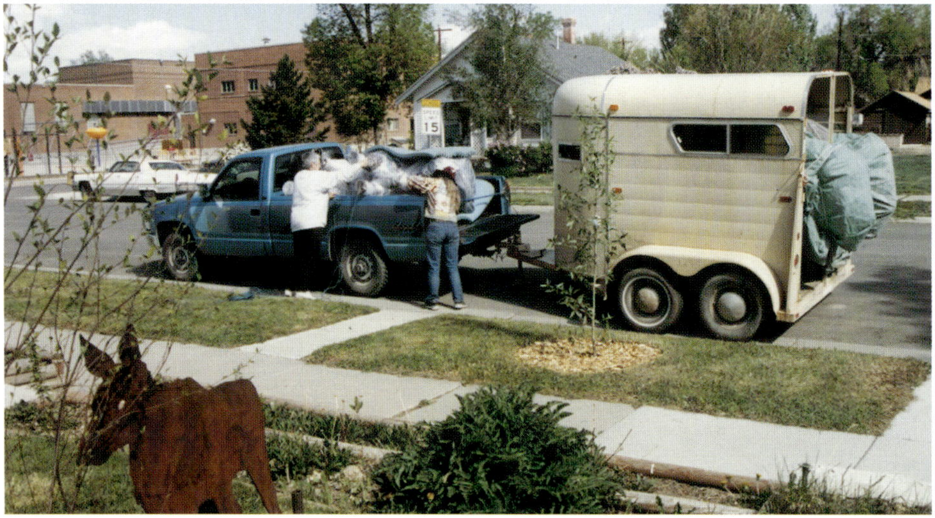

Photo: Elijah Cobb

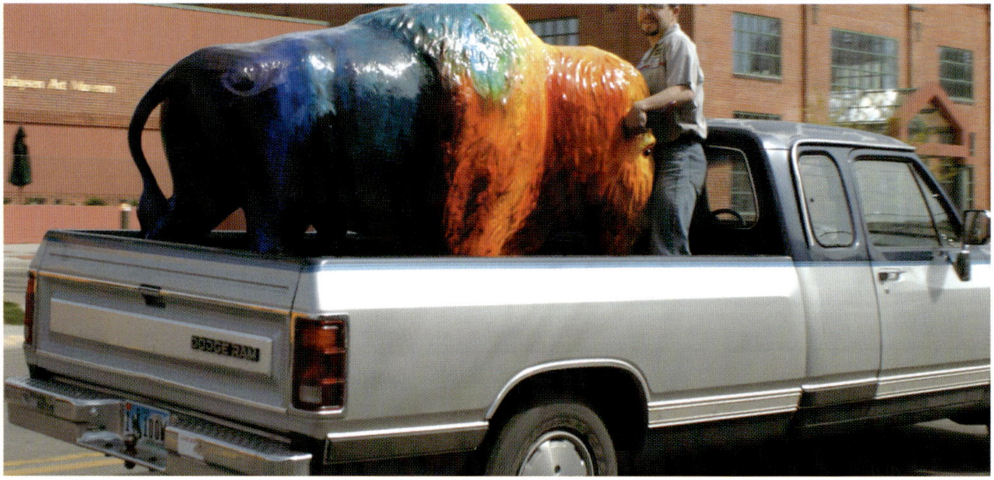

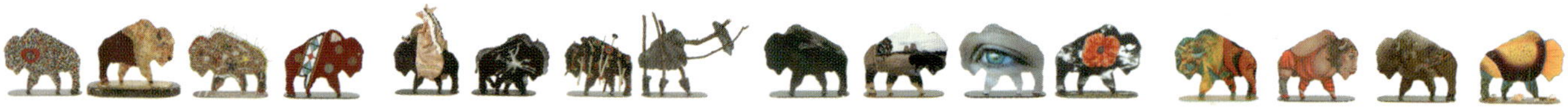

Next, all the Buffalo were sent out to pasture at sponsor locations for the summer with maps of the Buffalo's locations available statewide. The Buffalo adventure ends when they are rounded up one last time and herded to the grand finale and dinner on September 5th, sold at a live auction and transferred to their new homes.

And that's not all. There are, in addition, one hundred metal mini-Buffalo. These miniature works of art were painted by regional artists to also be offered for purchase during the final event. Other official Buffalo merchandise — books, t-shirts, posters and Buffalo related gifts — is available at the museum and at various retail outlets city wide.

What made this project so wonderful were the smiling, excited responses of the people as they viewed the Buffalo. They were petted, photographed, stroked and even hugged. Our community has really embraced these Buffalo and they have caused people to think about art in a new way. Art, of course, is about breaking down barriers and people saw this art as fun...something for everyone and very accessible.

Where the Buffalo Roam brings our community together. We relate and talk to strangers, make new friends and declare a common ground. All of us will surely remember with pleasure the summer of 2003 when the Buffalo roamed in Casper.

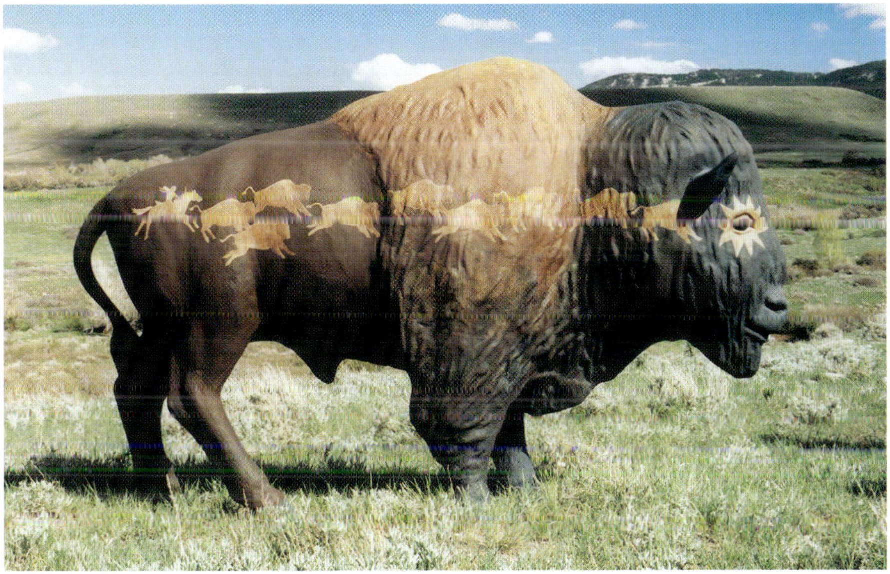

Photo: Chris Navarro

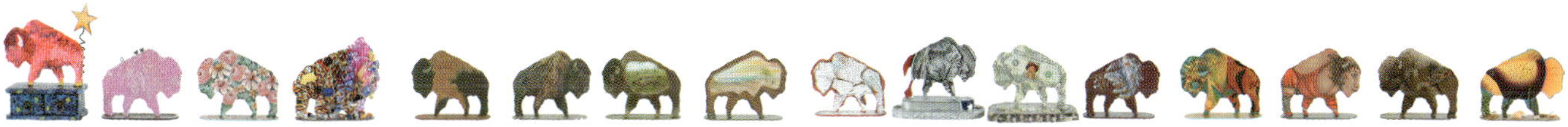

Edie Reno

WYOMING SONGS

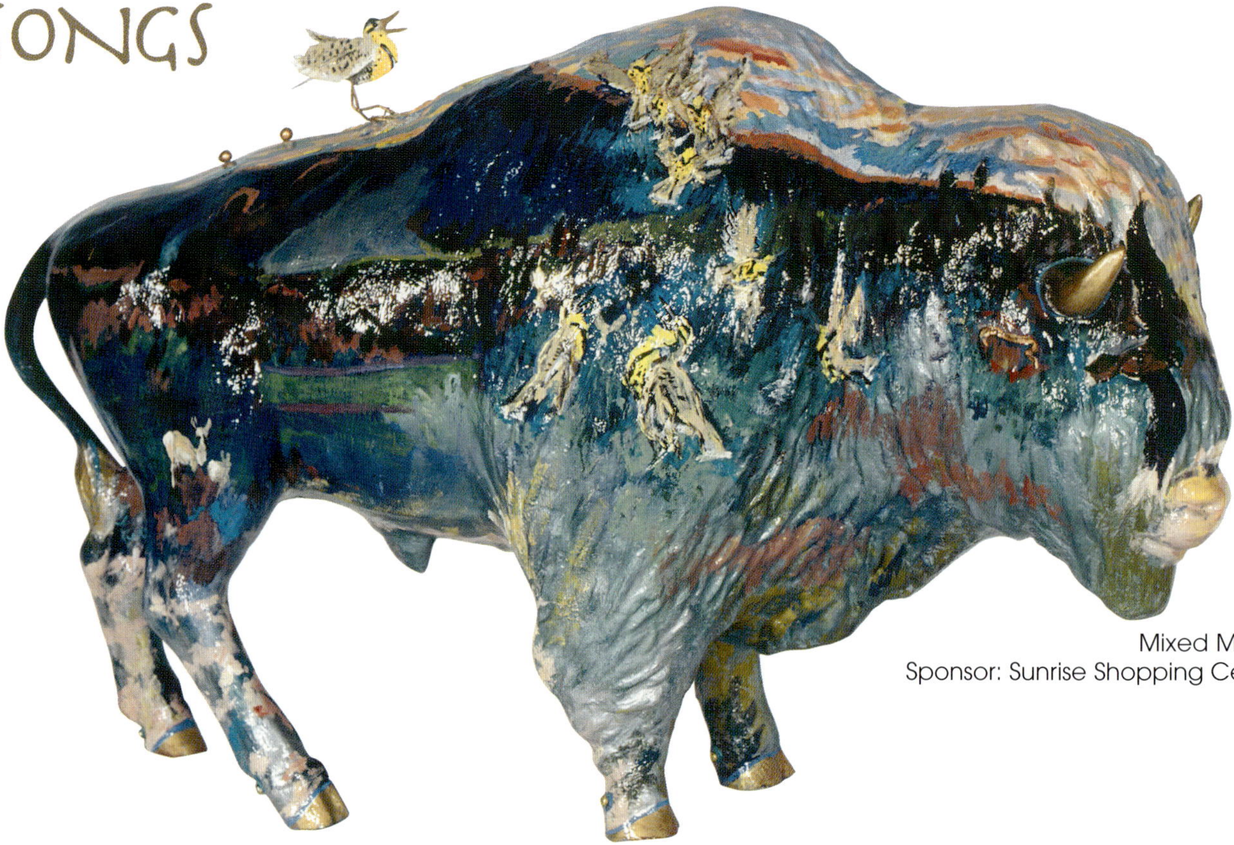

Mixed Media
Sponsor: Sunrise Shopping Center

"The 'Last Blue Hour' and its light plus the sounds at that time of day were my inspiration. I also have a horse in Sheridan this year for the *Herd is the Word* project there.

"I've shown around the West and internationally over a 25 year period. 'Ranch tech' is my current genre."

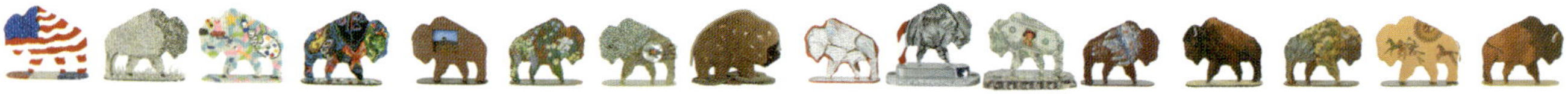

Theodore Waddell

POLLOCK'S BUFFALO

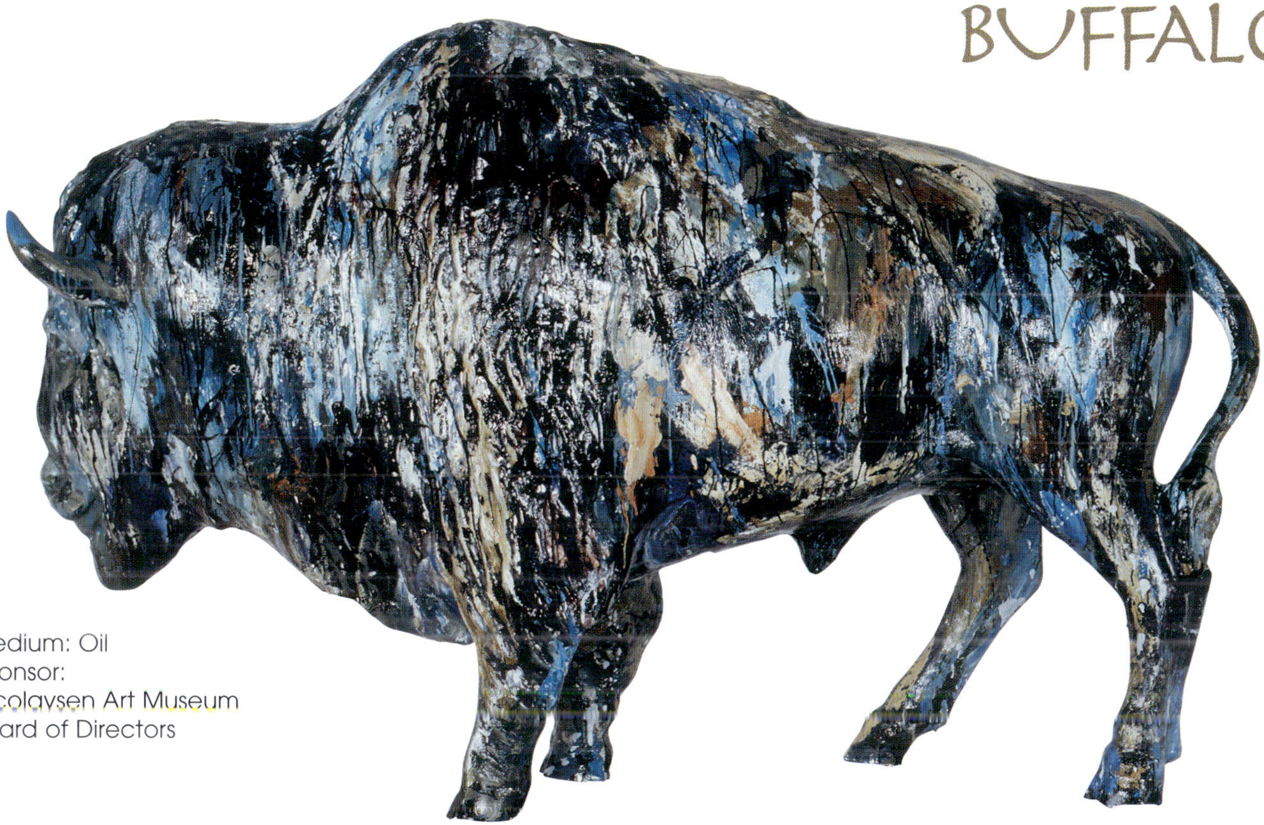

Medium: Oil
Sponsor:
Nicolaysen Art Museum
Board of Directors

Ted Waddell cites Jackson Pollock as his inspiration. Pollock was born in Cody, Wyoming. Ted is a native of Montana and currently divides his time between Montana and Idaho. His work is in private, corporate and museum collections throughout the country.

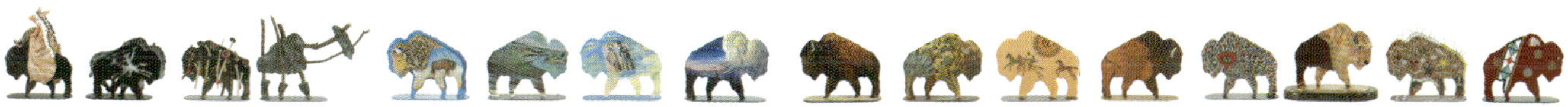

Sonja Huff, Nancy Stroh & Karen Henneck

ART HISTORY 101

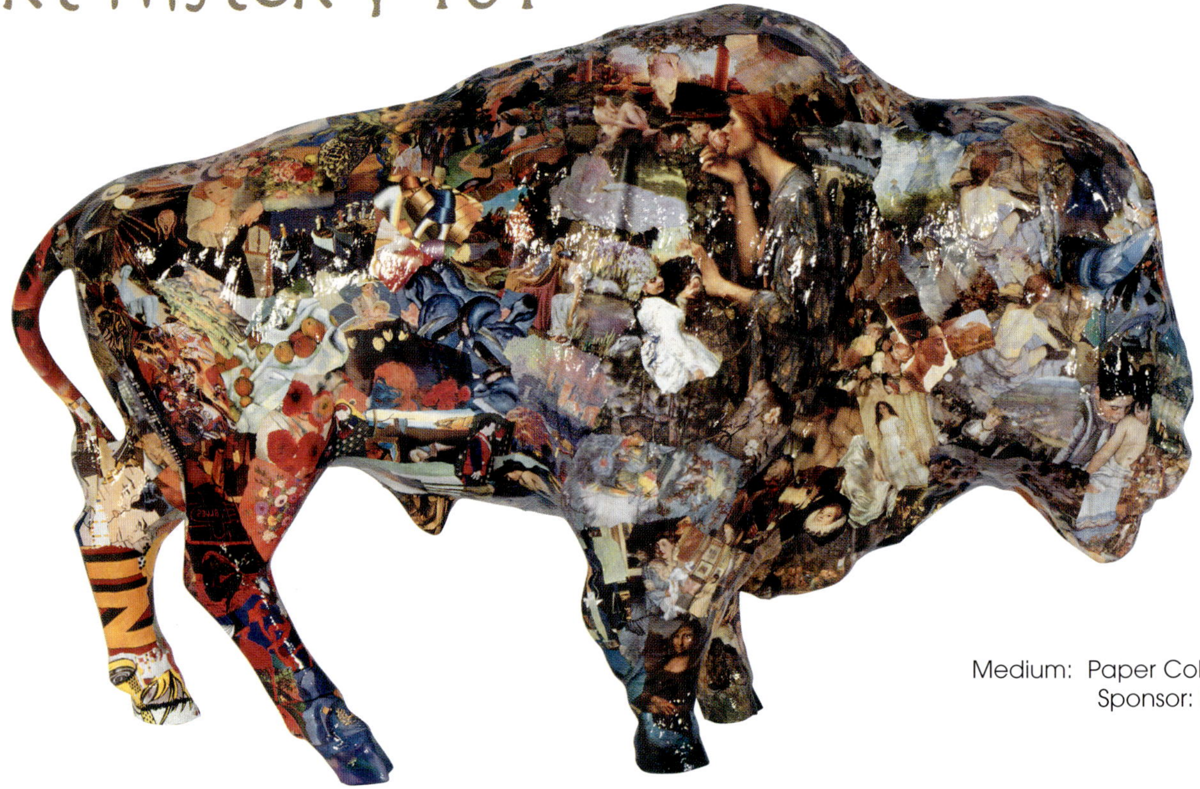

Medium: Paper Collage
Sponsor: K2TV

"Our inspiration for the Buffalo is the evolution of art throughout the ages, which has inspired us to express our own creativity and spirituality. We are friends who met at Casper College while pursuing our art education. As the impressionists met, shared and encouraged each other, so do we. We have a special group that meets and critiques on a regular basis. Our art is enhanced by the relationships we have with each other."

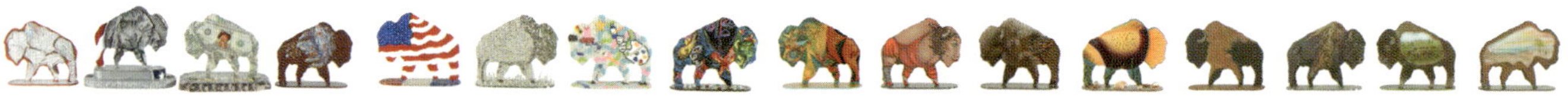

Debra Hall & Patti Gingles

LEWIS & CLARK

ANNIVERSARY RENDITION

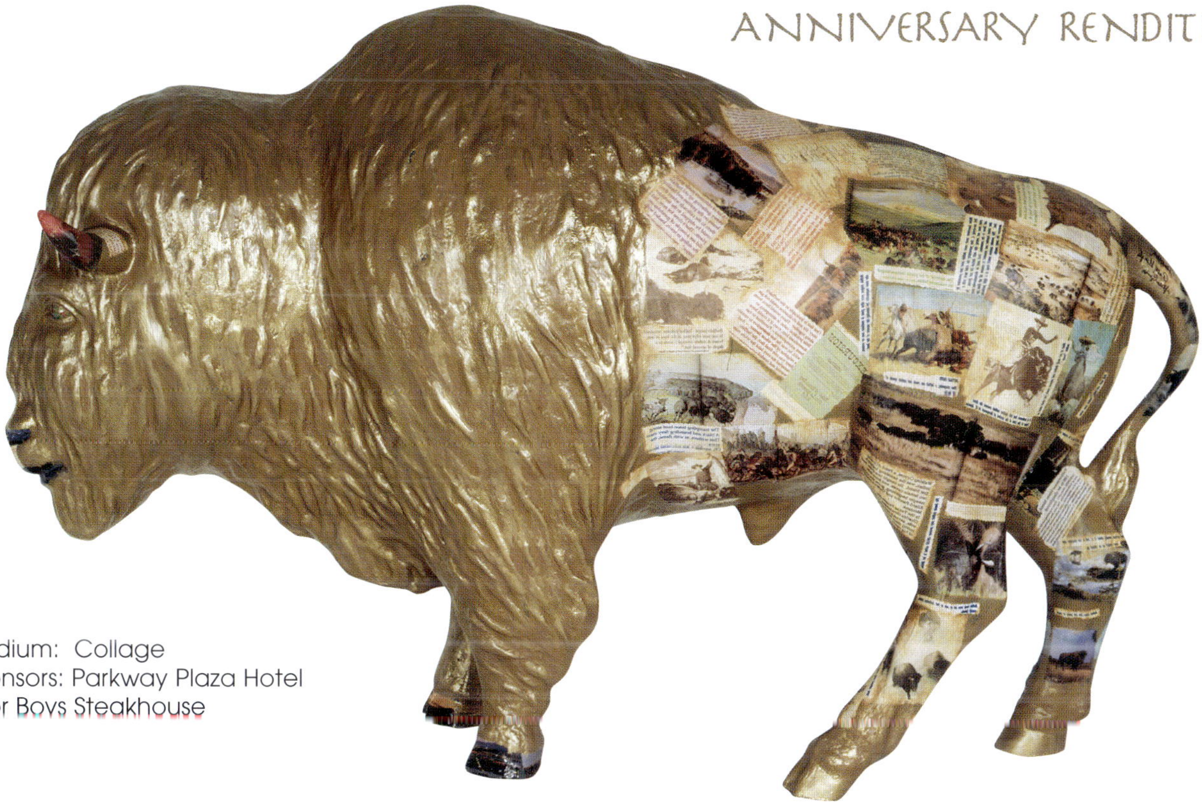

Medium: Collage
Sponsors: Parkway Plaza Hotel
Poor Boys Steakhouse

"The inspiration for this piece was a celebration of 100 years since Lewis & Clark"
Debra — a fused glass artist - nationally known, and Patti good friend — did research & both worked on the Buffalo.

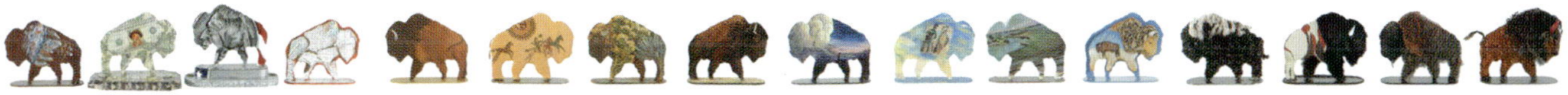

B.J. Durr
TRIBUTE TO THE BUFFALO

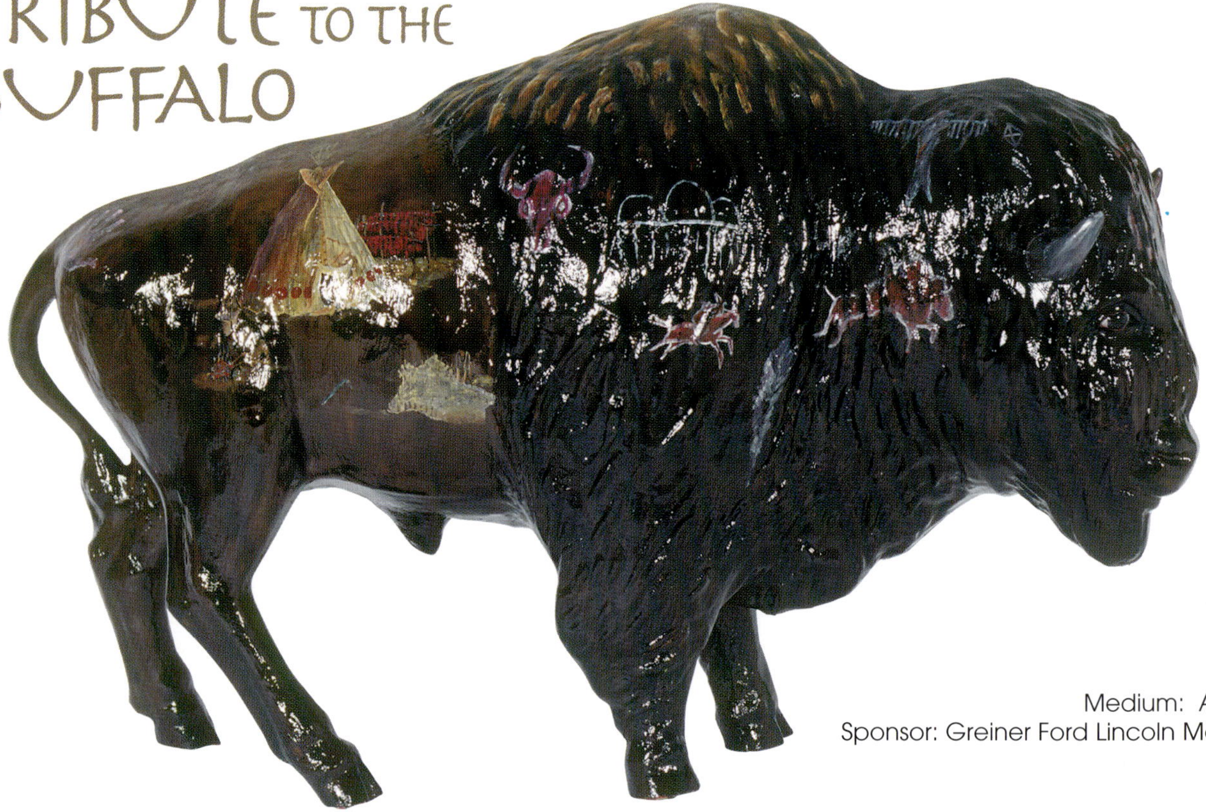

Medium: Acrylic
Sponsor: Greiner Ford Lincoln Mercury

"The magnificent animal himself, the history of his existence and my own interest in Indian history and Wyoming history all served as inspiration. I was continually amazed at how this Buffalo — (whose name is 'krackatoa'!) was turning out, the interest shown by friends and local entities in his size — and progress — plus the Wyoming Watercolor Society attendees when they 'visited'. He's even been blessed by our Mayor and I, too, am blessed for this opportunity!
"FYI — mine was the 'cracked' one returned to the factory, and when I'd finished my 'airbrush coat' I dropped the paint sprayer on my toe, thus — Krackatoa.' The amazement of the Fed Ex man, when delivering a package — 'Did you know there's a Buffalo out there?'— added to the fun!"

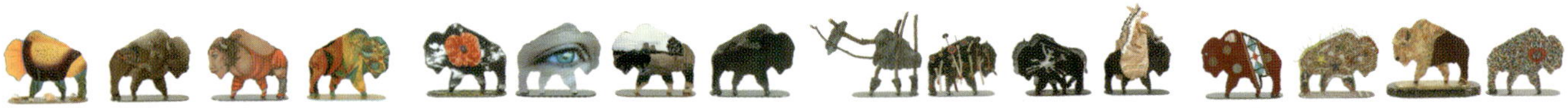

Linda Lillegraven

EMERGING FROM THE PLEISTOCENE

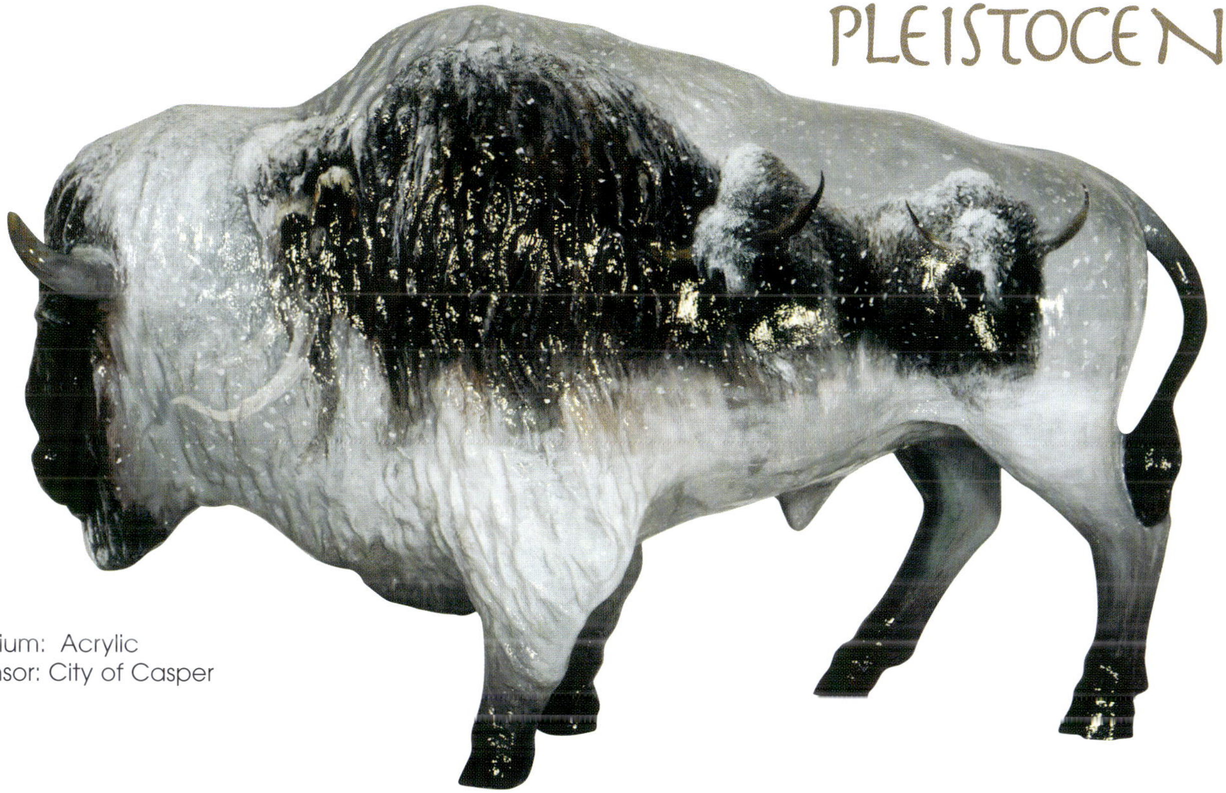

Medium: Acrylic
Sponsor: City of Casper

"Looking out onto a snowy Wyoming landscape always makes me feel we're not far removed from the last Ice Age. The bison was well-adapted then as now. I show him with the memory of the great herds that once roamed this place, in summer and winter.

"I like to paint the vast, free, uncomfortable, joyous, intimidating open spaces of Wyoming. I had a one person show at the Nic in 1999-2000."

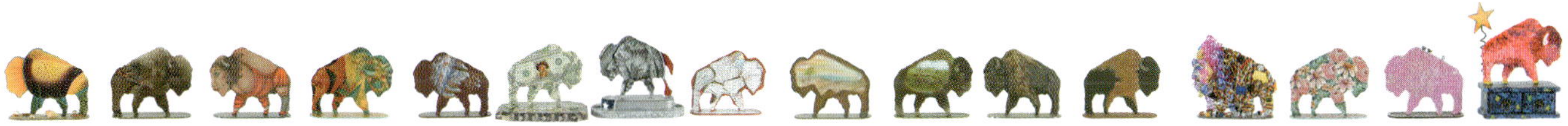

Linda L. Ryan

WHITE BUFFALO

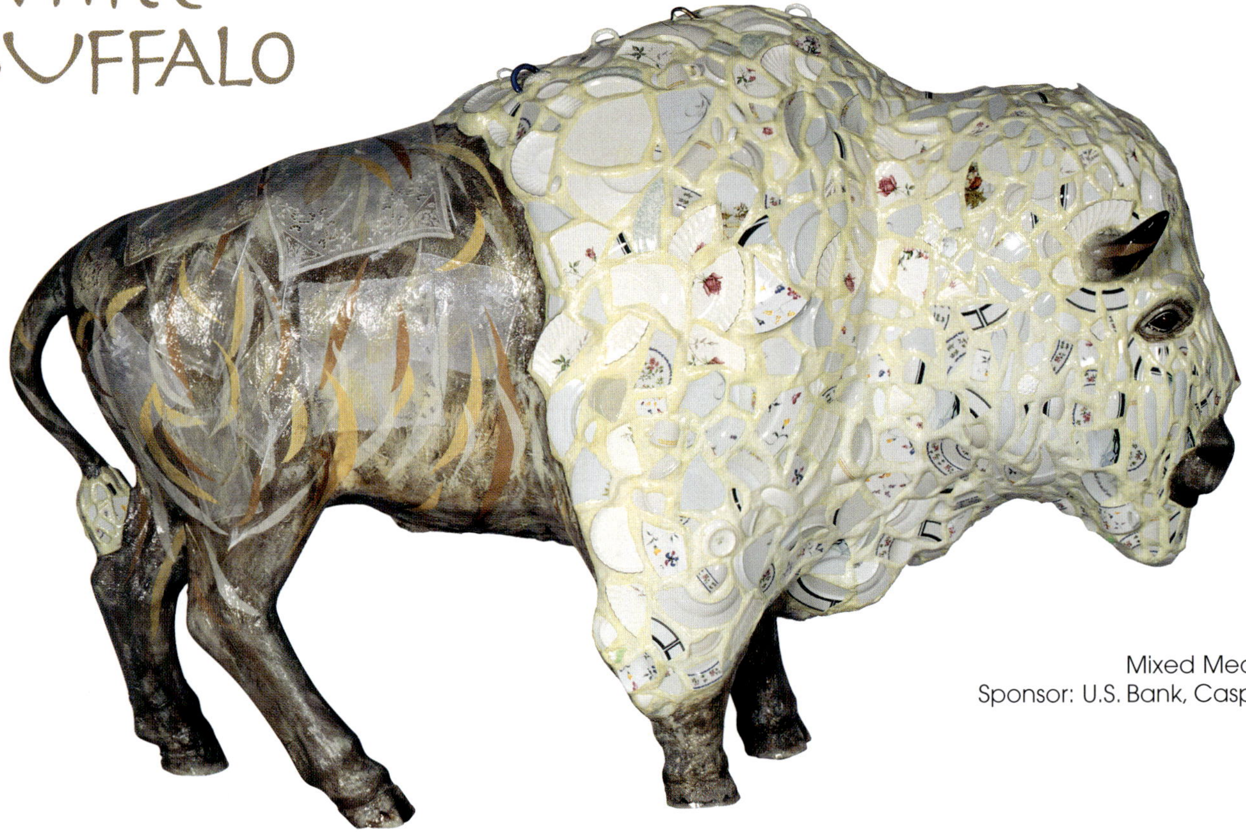

Mixed Media
Sponsor: U.S. Bank, Casper

"The Inspiration is the legend of the holy woman who appeared to the Lakota people bringing the sacred pipe. After she taught the mysteries of living and following a proper path, she walked away, rolled on the ground, and became a white Buffalo calf. The Buffalo has since become a symbol of sacred life and abundance.

"I used domestic materials such as hankies, fabric and lace and broken white porcelain dishes to suggest a white female Buffalo. On the inside I have placed prayer ties; bundles into which people have prayed and offered blessings."

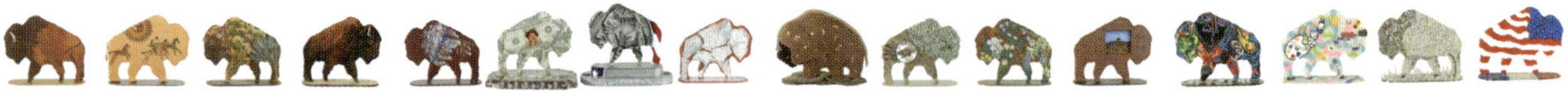

John Giarrizzo

DISTANT THUNDER

IN RED AND BLACK

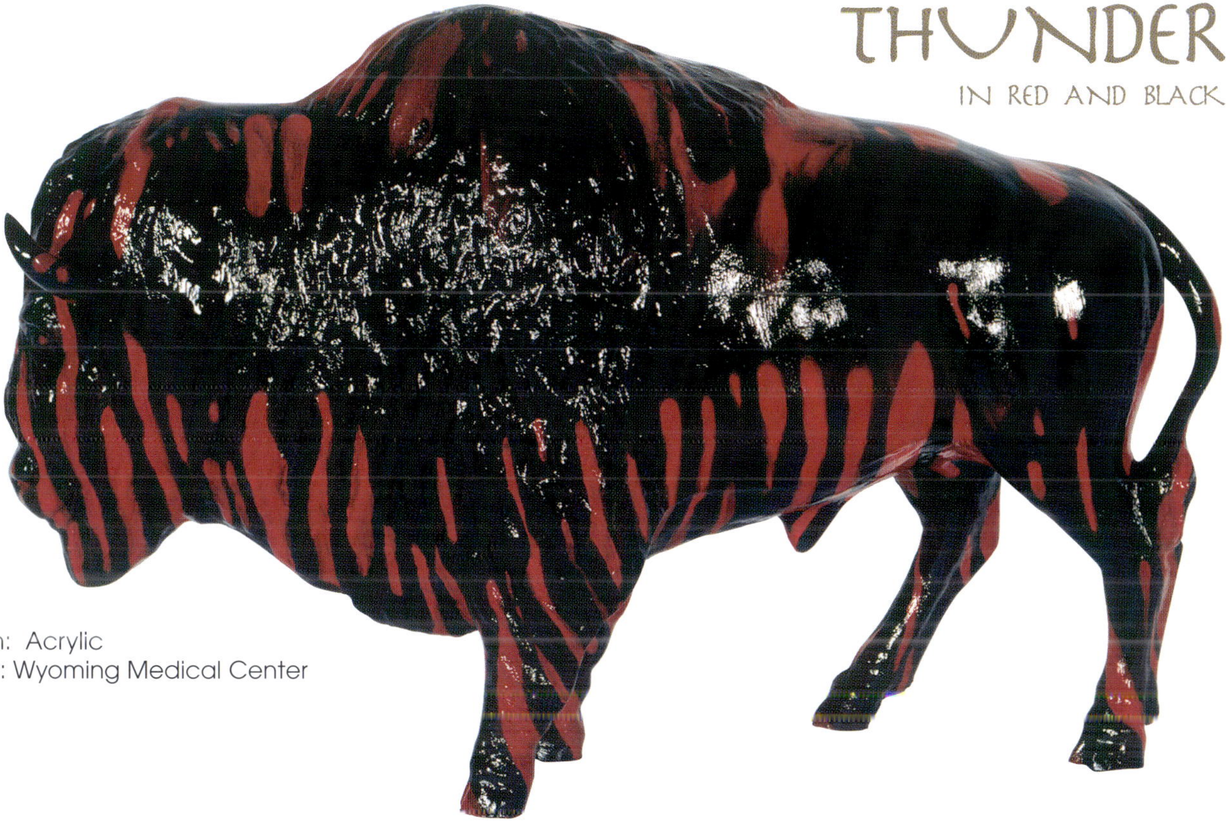

Medium: Acrylic
Sponsor: Wyoming Medical Center

"The Red Desert series is a recent body of work paying homage to the wild horses of the Red Desert." John Giarrizzo has taught drawing and painting at Northwest College since 1981. 2002 recipient of the Governor's Award in the Arts, he is also recipient of Wyoming Arts Council fellowships in 1987 and 1992, and the 2002 Kim Baer Award in Painting.

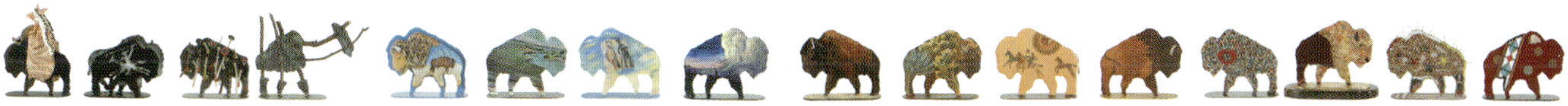

Lynn Thorpe

SYNONYMOUS

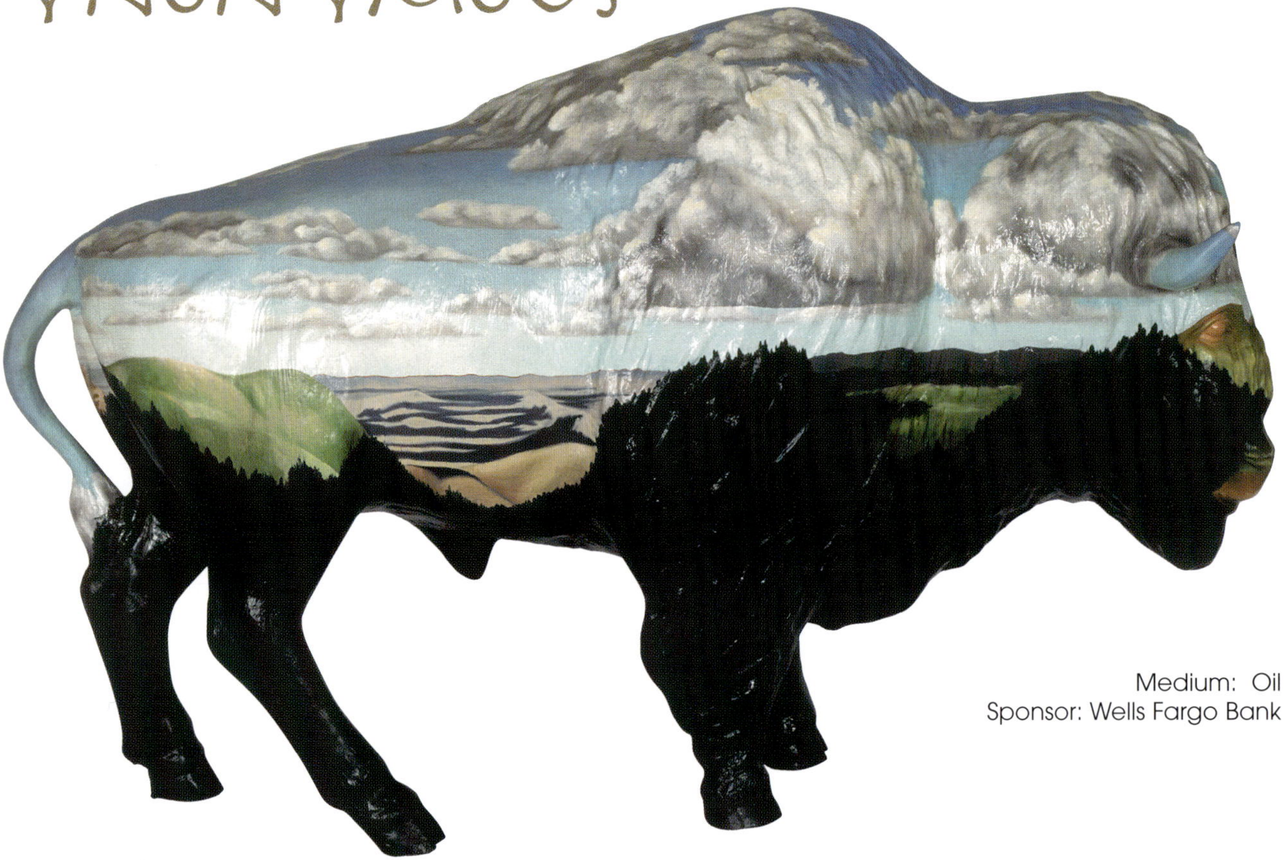

Medium: Oil
Sponsor: Wells Fargo Bank

"My relationship to the Wyoming landscape prompted the idea. The concept solidified when I realized that placed outdoors, in the landscape & viewed from the right angle, the bison 'disappears.' This project turns wildlife painting inside out!"

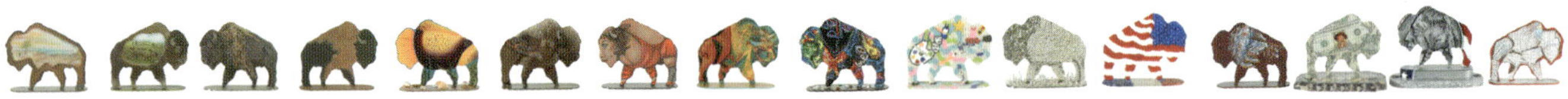

Linda Raynolds

MOTHER OF MILLIONS

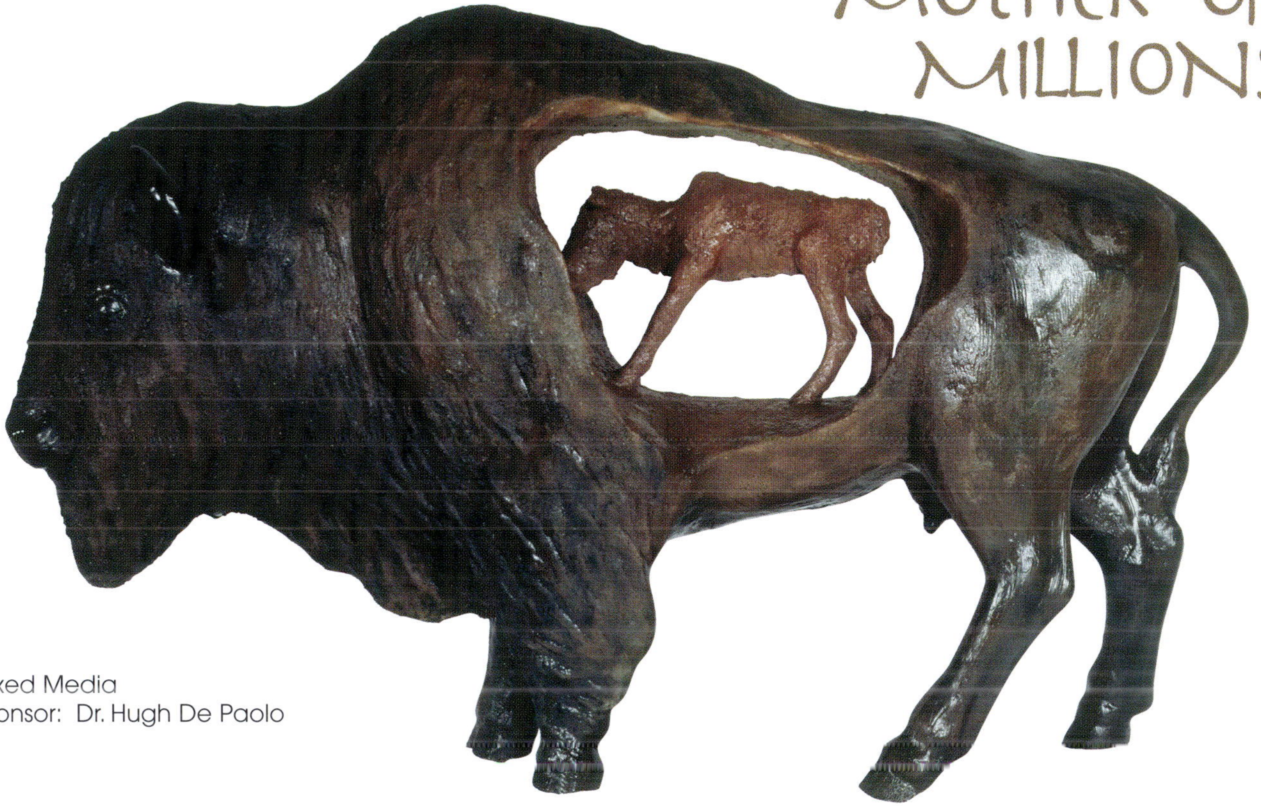

Mixed Media
Sponsor: Dr. Hugh De Paolo

"The Buffalo is a survivor. Just as there were millions of Buffalo in the past, there will be millions of Buffalo again in the future. This matriarch, daughter of an unbroken lineage of matriarchs, carries her calf into the 21st century.
"My parents have been Buffalo ranchers south of Lander for more than 25 years."

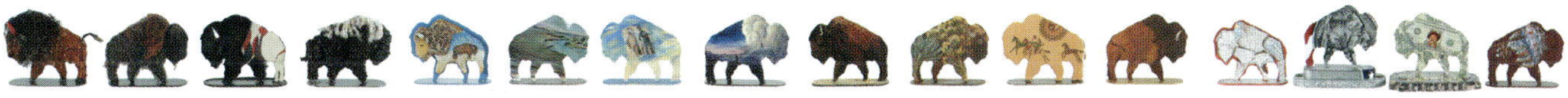

Chris Navarro

BUFFALO SPIRIT

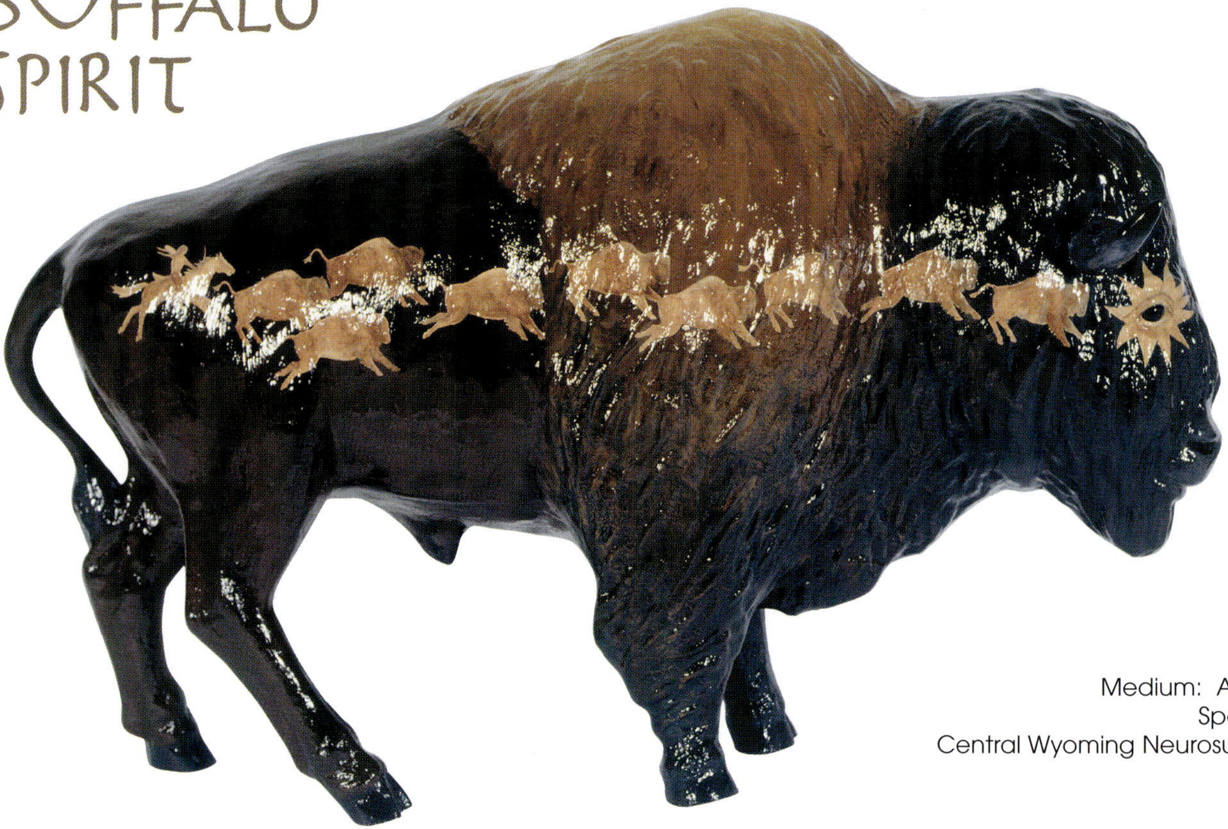

Medium: Acrylic
Sponsor:
Central Wyoming Neurosurgery

"The Buffalo was life to the Plains Indians. They put every part of the Buffalo to use. The Indians believed everything spiritually and materially was contained within the Buffalo. No other animal ever gave so much to a people as the great shaggy Buffalo.

"I have been a professional artist for seventeen years working in bronze, creating small to monumental sculptures. I feel very fortunate to live in Wyoming and blessed to make a living doing what I love."

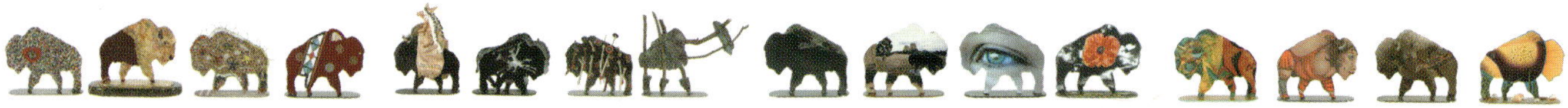

Jen Champlin

SHARDS IN SAND

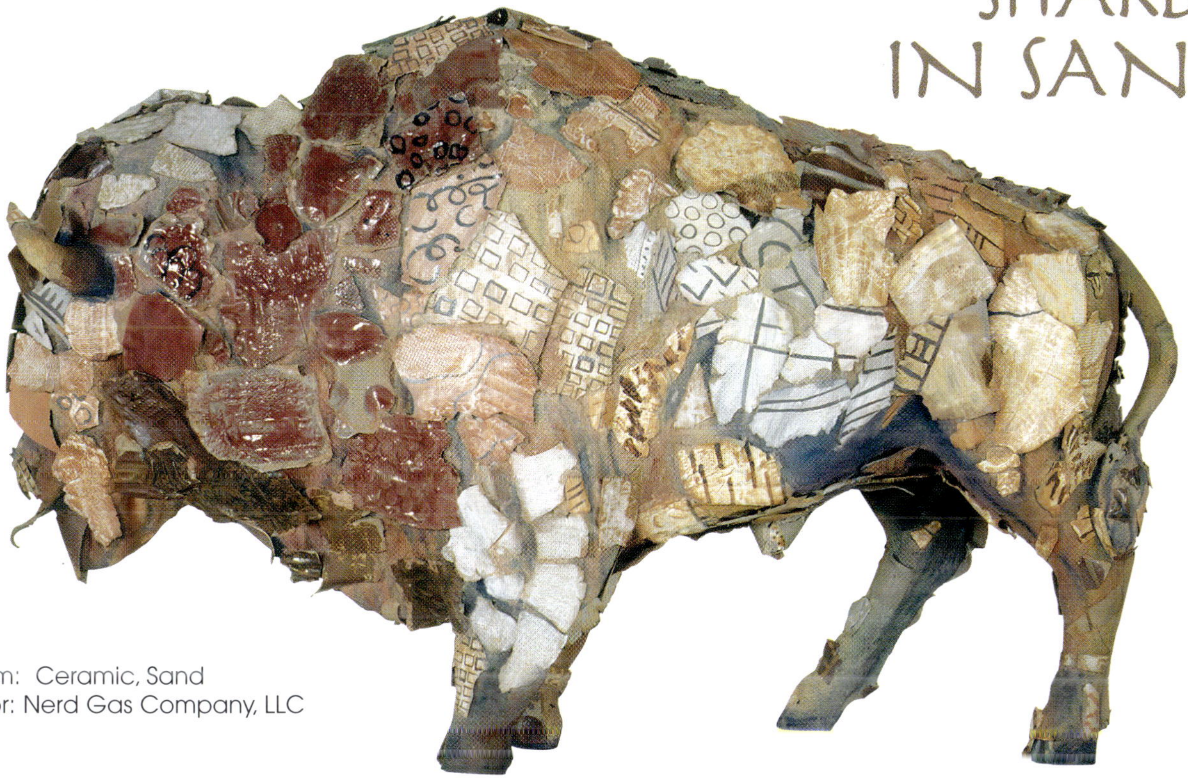

Medium: Ceramic, Sand
Sponsor: Nerd Gas Company, LLC

"My husband's grandfather 'legally' harvested hundreds of ceramic shards from the Santa Fe area. I love studying these relics. I'm amazed by their detail, shape, profile, and cross-sections. This Buffalo is made from my interpretation of these shards."

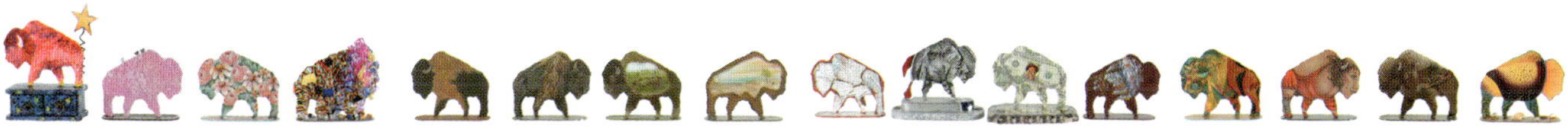

The Wyoming Watercolor Company

THE LUV BUFF

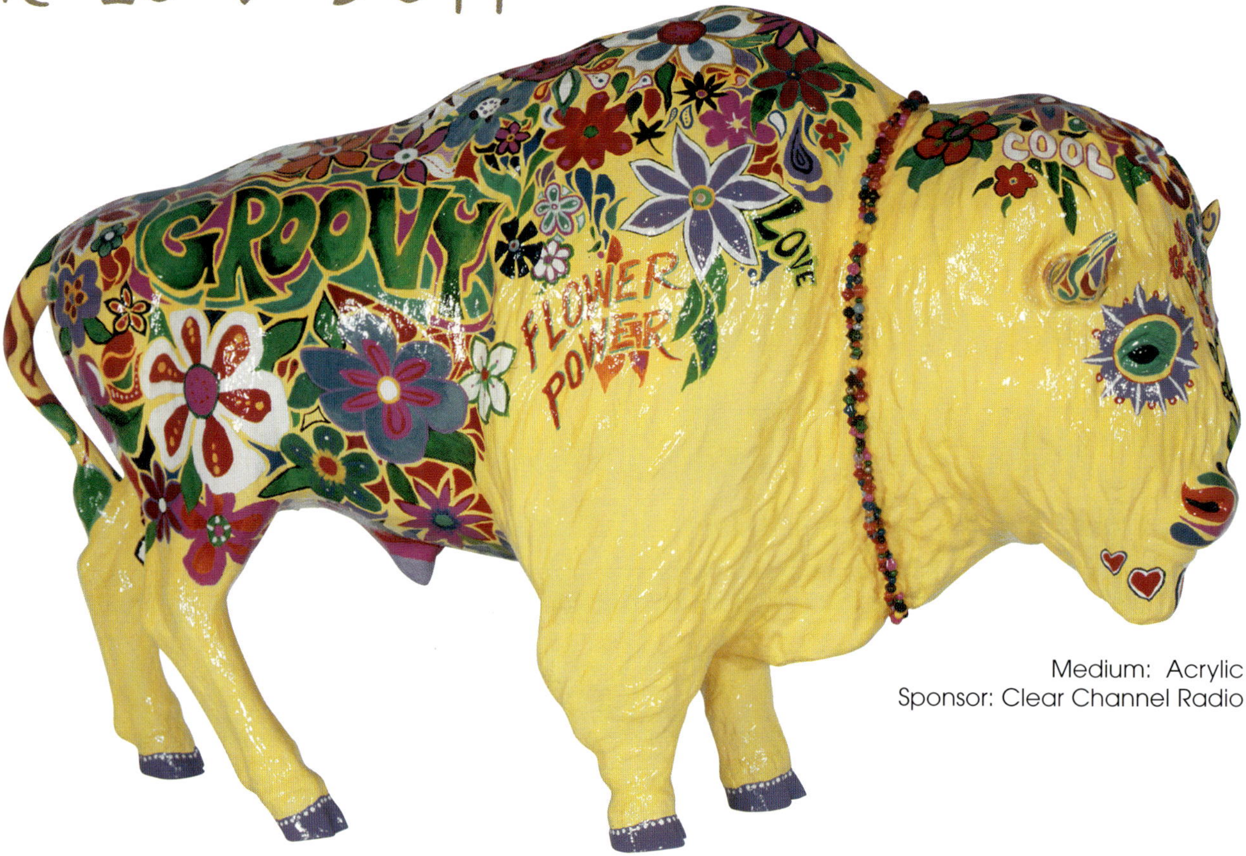

Medium: Acrylic
Sponsor: Clear Channel Radio

"Our inspiration for this project stems from a reflection of the 60's "flower power" style. As flower children decorated their vans, clothing and their bodies, we chose to duplicate this approach with the Buffalo. Our 'LUV BUFF' with its bright floral patterns reflects the appreciation we all share for the flora and fauna of our state."

The Watercolor Company is a professional group of six Casper, Wyoming artists: Holly Bishop, Jim Gaither, Skip Larcom, Barbara Kuxhausen, Michele McDonald and Joan Melius. The artists exhibit their work as a collective presentation of individual approaches to the watercolor medium.

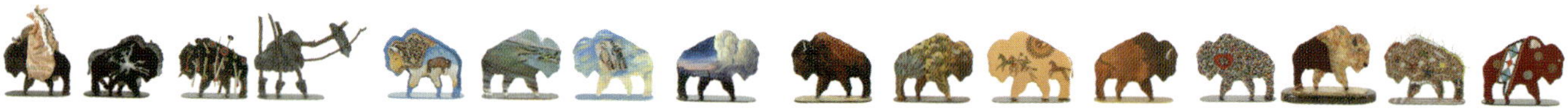

Dennis Cumin

BLUFFING BUFFALO

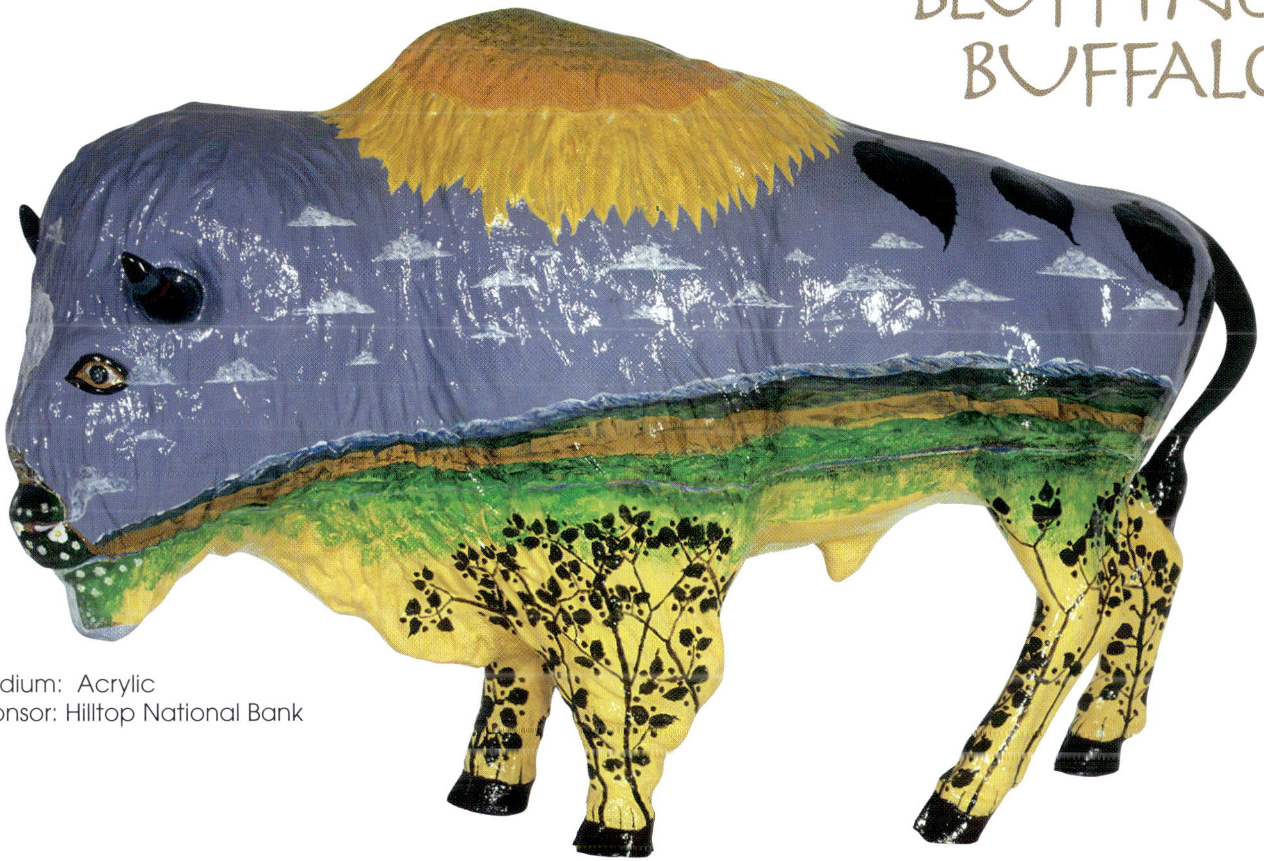

Medium: Acrylic
Sponsor: Hilltop National Bank

"The high and low mountain plains of Wyoming and Montana served as inspiration. I have researched a lot of antique art processes along with new high tech processes and continue to use them in my art work."

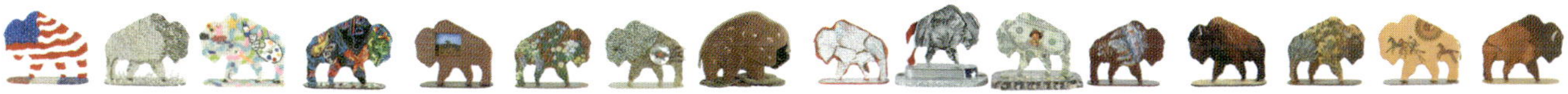

Kevin Red Star & Sunny Sky

PROVIDER OF THE PLAINS INDIANS

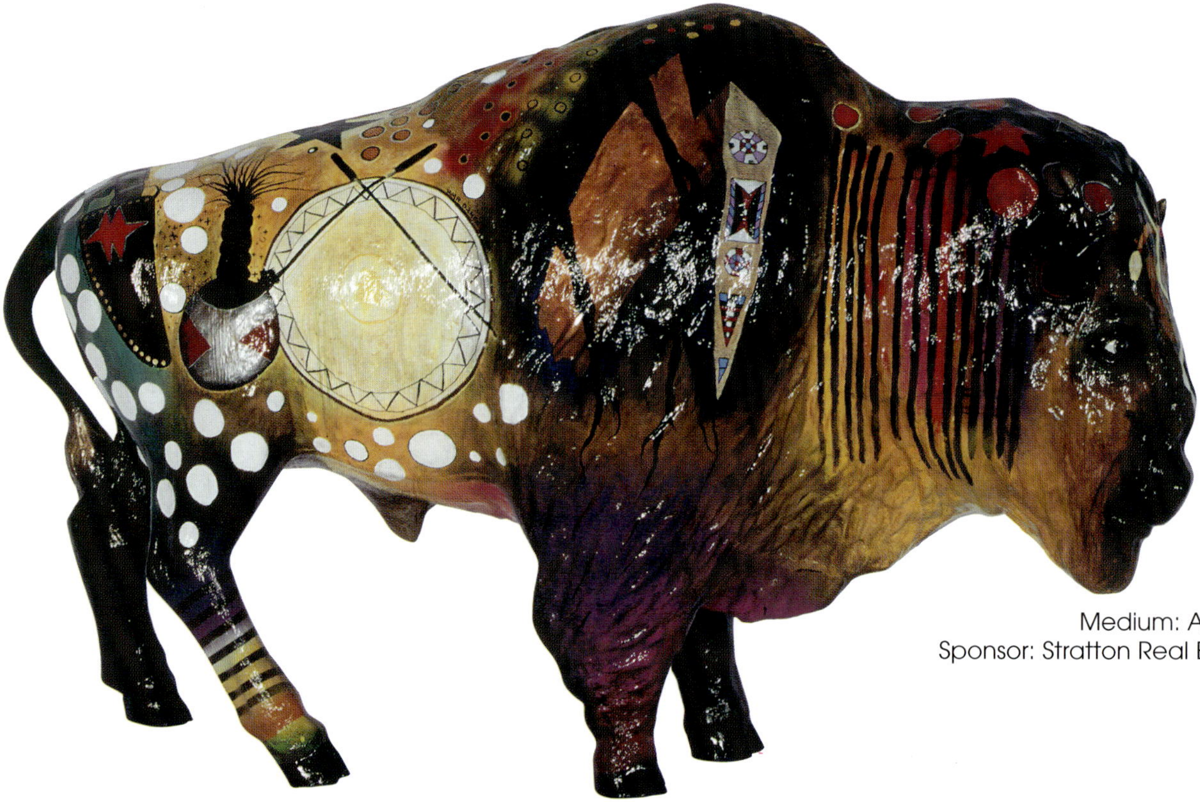

Medium: Acrylic
Sponsor: Stratton Real Estate

Kevin Red Star has emerged as the premier Northern Plains fine artist. When he became serious about his art, he studied and experimented with color and techniques of the Masters until his style evolved. One can always identify "Red Star" but his growth as an artist and person never stops, much to the delight of his collectors and fans. His philosophy parallels Robert Rauschenberg's: "There should be no barriers in art."

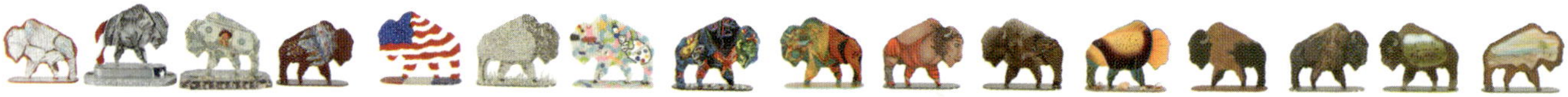

Tom Loepp

NICOLO

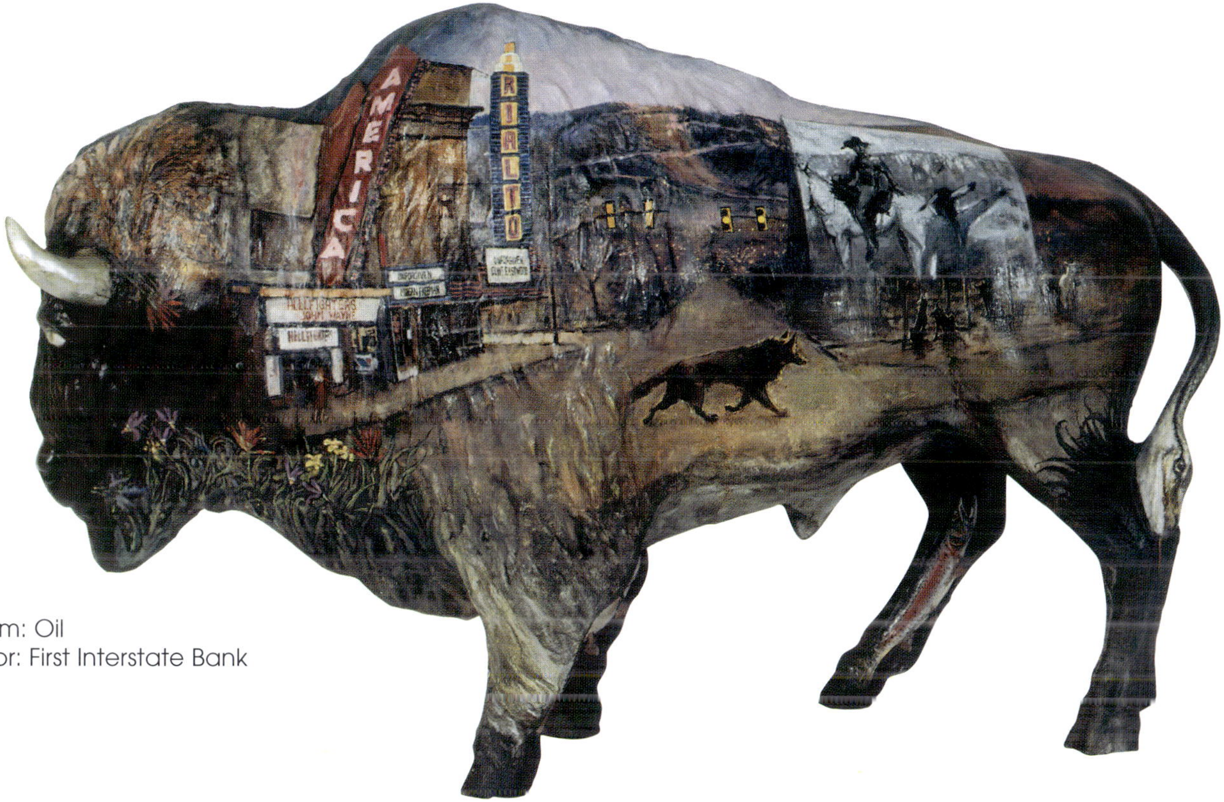

Medium: Oil
Sponsor: First Interstate Bank

"I used the lines and form of the bison to somewhat shape the concept and develop the design. I drew Inspiration from Casper Mountain, the Platte River and landscapes including the downtown area.
"In my art I have taken `so what' to its highest form."

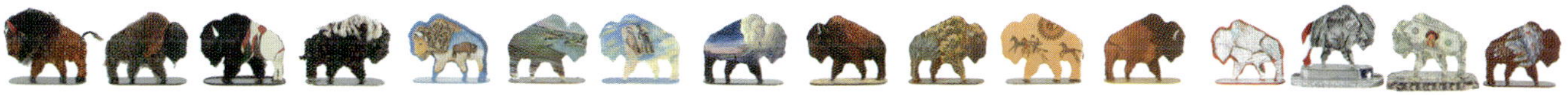

Joe Arnold
YELLOWSTONE BUFFALO

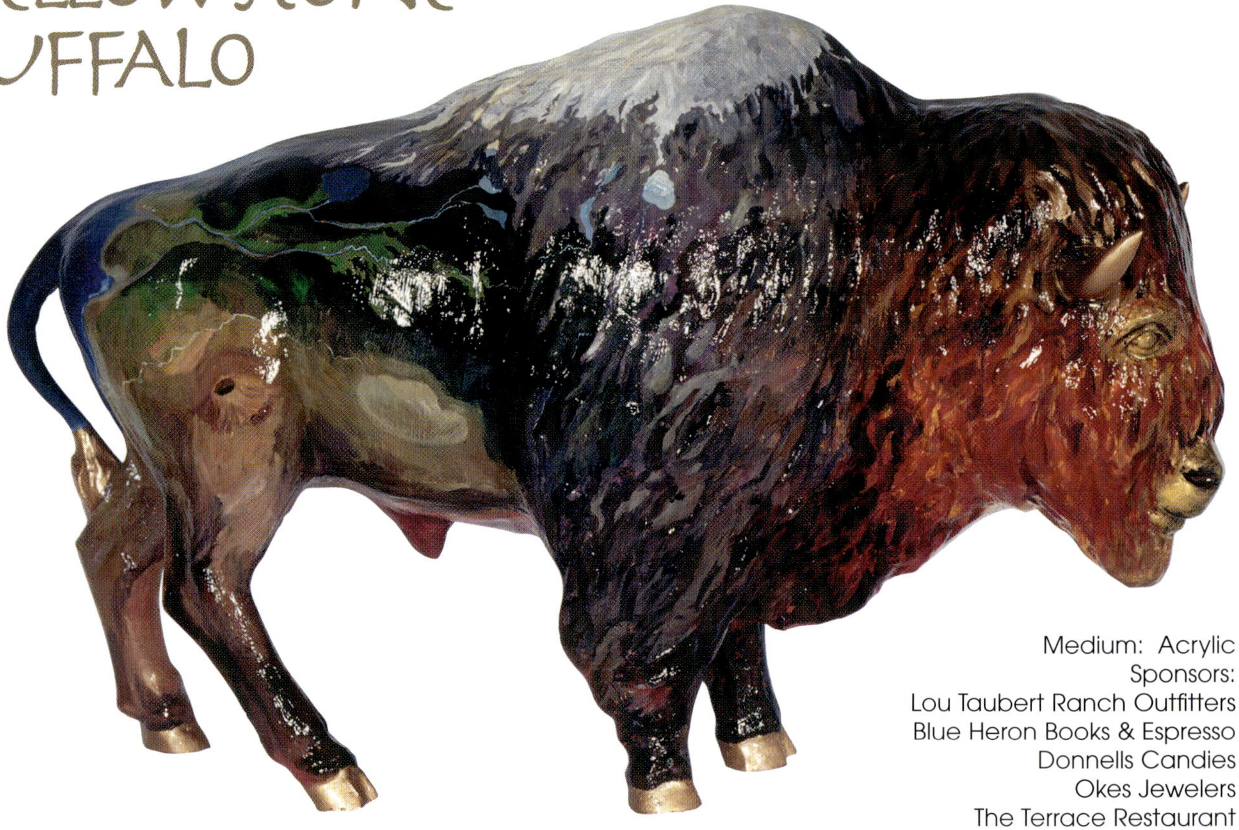

Medium: Acrylic
Sponsors:
Lou Taubert Ranch Outfitters
Blue Heron Books & Espresso
Donnells Candies
Okes Jewelers
The Terrace Restaurant
All Rock Mortgage Company

"I had in mind the elements that shaped the Yellowstone Ecosystem. The head is the fire of molten lava and the forest fires. The hump shows the glacial activity. Towards the back are the streams, forests and lakes. The fire in the belly reminds us that Yellowstone will erupt again.

"As a landscape painter for thirty years I enjoyed treating the Buffalo Project in a conceptual manner. Rather than a flat canvas with traditional perspective I had to use orthographic perspective, as in a map."

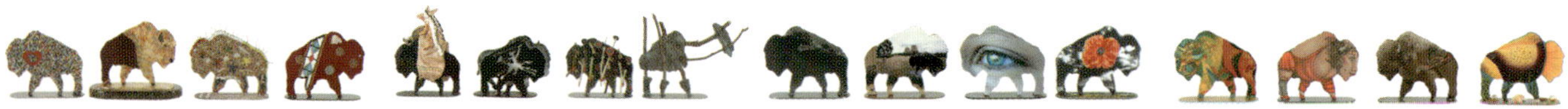

Kathryn Yauney
BUFFALO PEOPLE

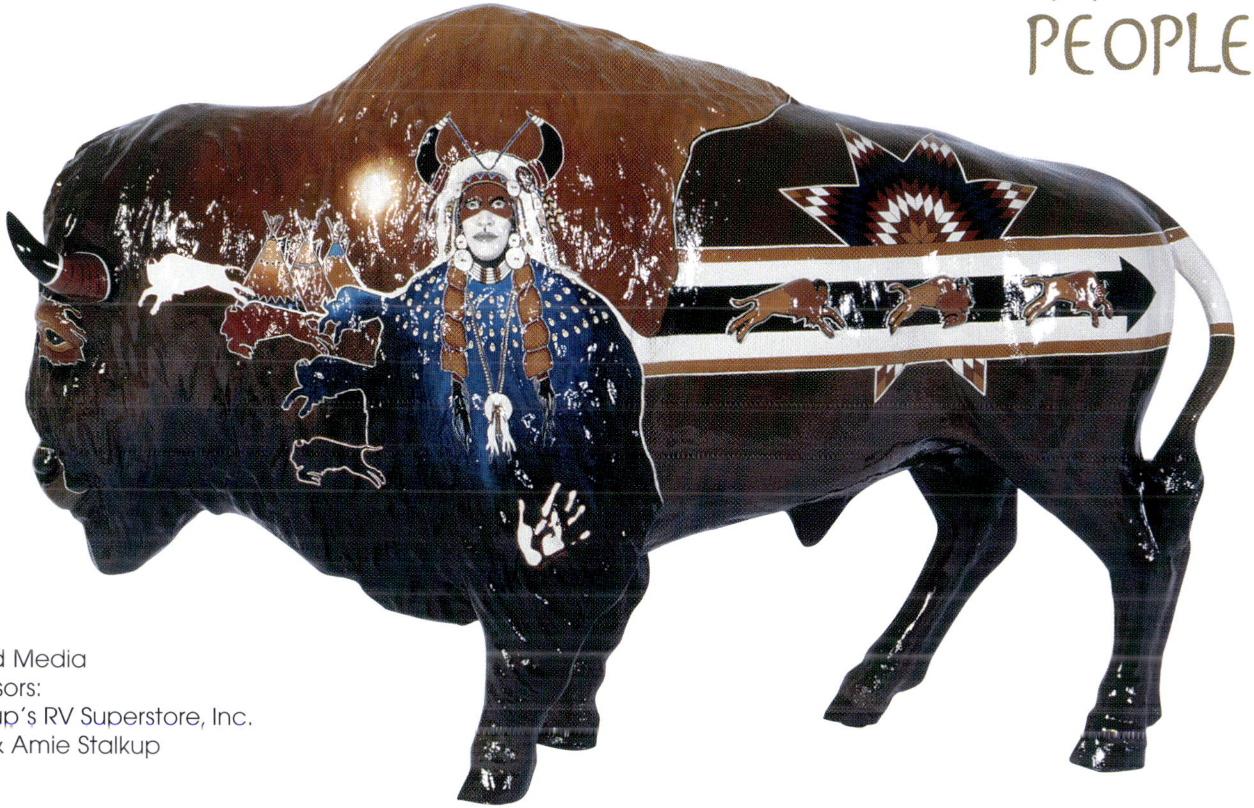

Mixed Media
Sponsors:
Stalkup's RV Superstore, Inc.
Ray & Amie Stalkup

"The Buffalo was life to the Plains Indian. No other animal gave so much to a people. This included their food, shelter, clothing and even their religious beliefs. The Plains Indians truly were the 'Buffalo People.' "Living in Wyoming and being of native descent I have always felt a real quality with the Ancients of our area. Although I am a sculptor I have enjoyed the process of painting my ideas."

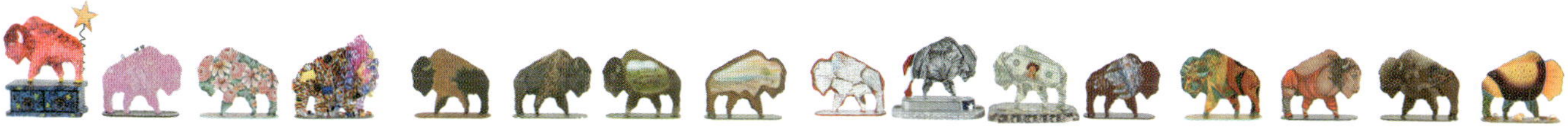

Ginny Butcher

"O, GIVE ME A HOME..."

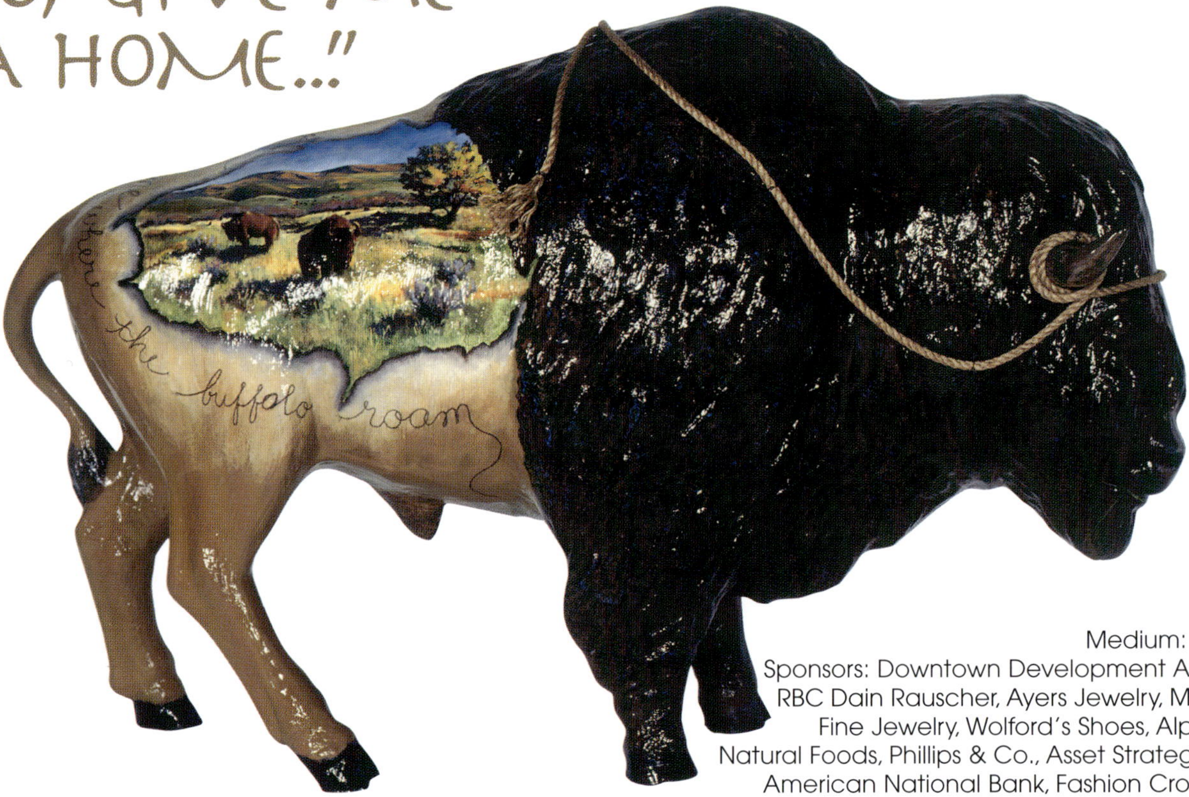

Medium: Acrylic
Sponsors: Downtown Development Authority, RBC Dain Rauscher, Ayers Jewelry, Michael's Fine Jewelry, Wolford's Shoes, Alpenglow Natural Foods, Phillips & Co., Asset Strategies Inc., American National Bank, Fashion Crossroads, Panos & Deuel Investments, LLC, Arch W. & Dana H. Deuel

"Wyoming's fresh beauty and untamed spaces — and the title of the fundraiser — were my source of inspiration.

"Asked for something interesting about myself, I offer the following: 1) I had a job selling bluegrass records at bluegrass festivals one summer. 2) I moved to Glendo from New Hampshire in 1980 to see what the West was like and, 3) I have painted for thirty plus years, but began professionally three years ago."

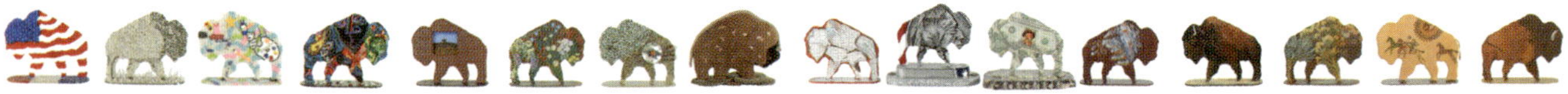

Annette Chaudet
BUFFALO ROBE

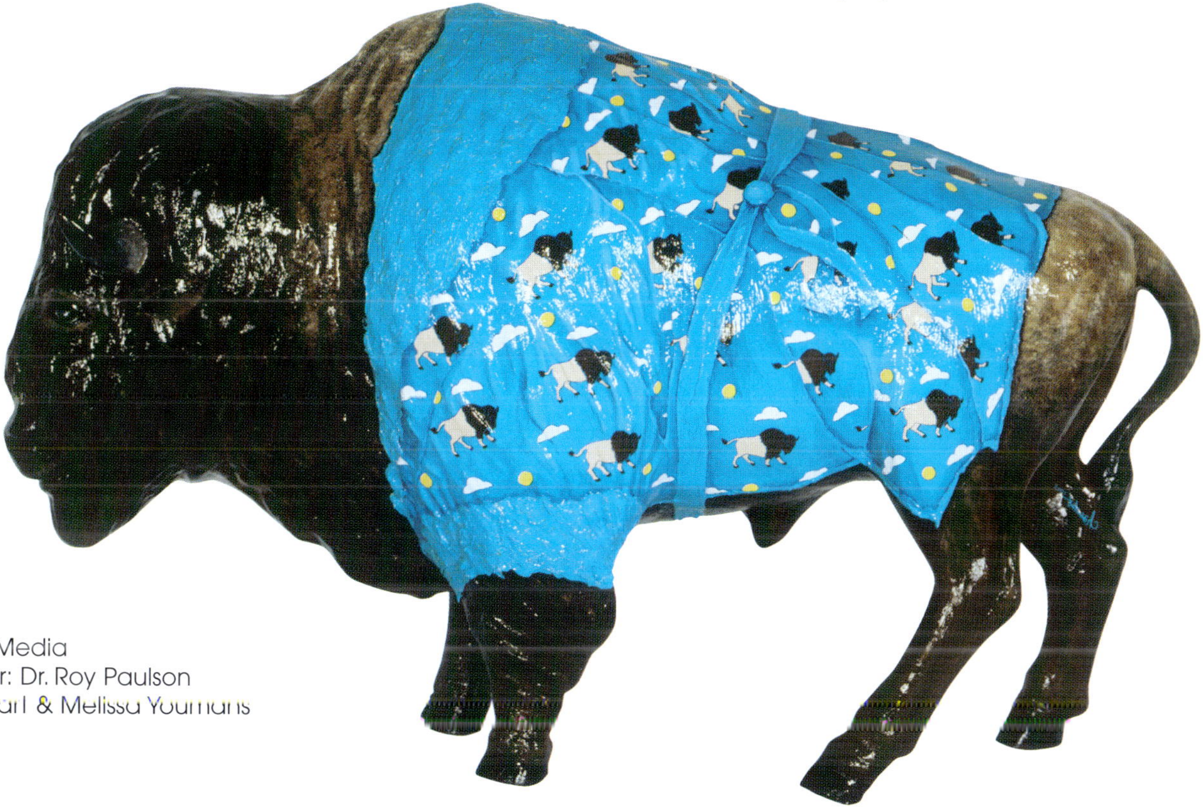

Mixed Media
Sponsor: Dr. Roy Paulson
Drs. Stuart & Melissa Youmans

"I began with the more serious and traditional concepts like 'White Buffalo', with images of herds on the great plains. Then I decided I wanted to have fun and began looking for a play on words but found 'Buffalo' somewhat limiting. When I started thinking 'Buffalo Robe' this image just kept on insisting there was no other choice!

"I have shown my work in many mediums all over the western states since the 1960s. My main focus in the realm of art in recent years has been flat cut steel sculpture. My publishing endeavor, Pronghorn Press, is demanding most of my time these days so I really enjoy the opportunity for an 'art break'!"

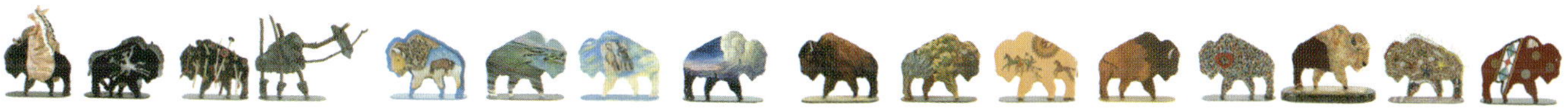

Robert Seabeck

BIG MIKE

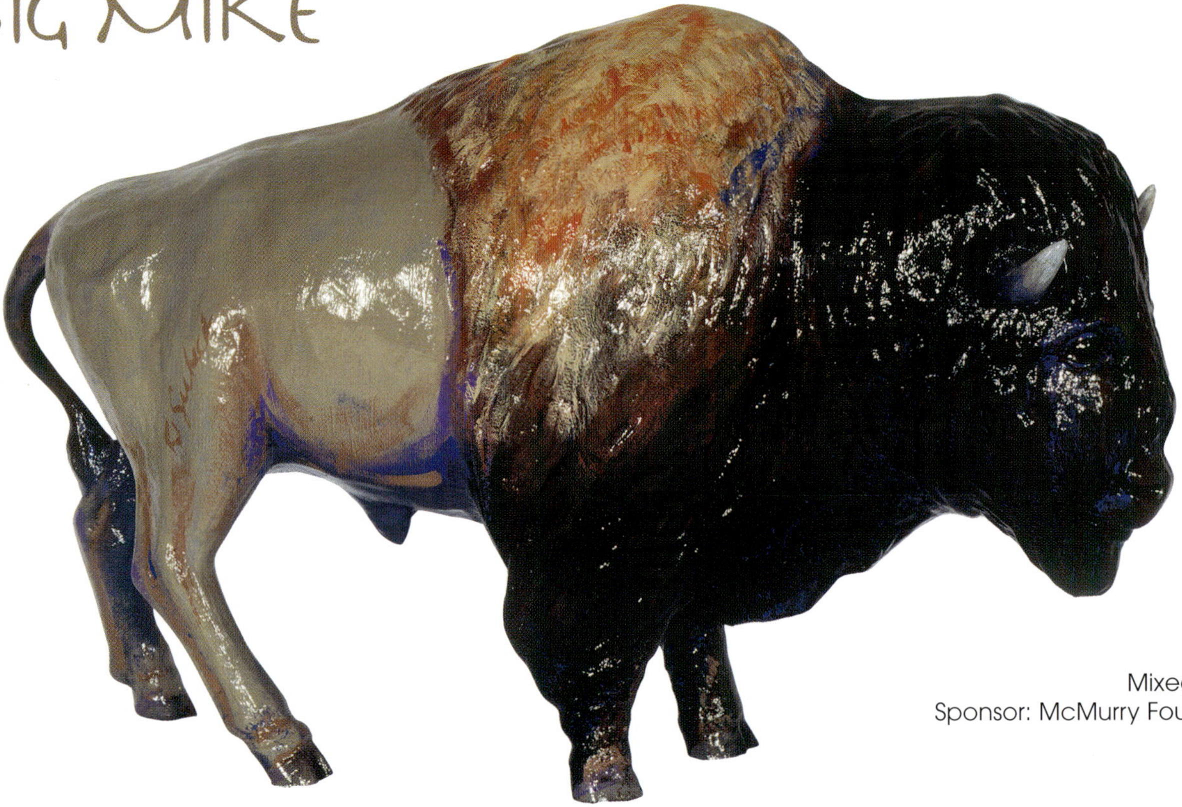

Mixed Media
Sponsor: McMurry Foundation

"My inspiration for this life size Buffalo is my personal admiration and excitement for this magnificent animal. Having painted this subject on flat surfaces for so long, in bold, intense colors — I suddenly had the opportunity to paint three dimensionally and life size! I look forward to working this size again.
"This painting started with three bold, intense colors; purple, orange and blue. The painting process built upon these three colors and proceeded towards this finished piece."

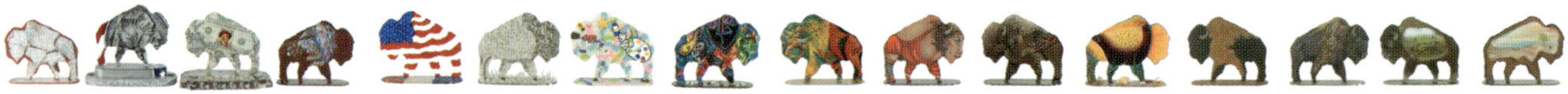

Sharon Merschat
CALL OF THE WILD

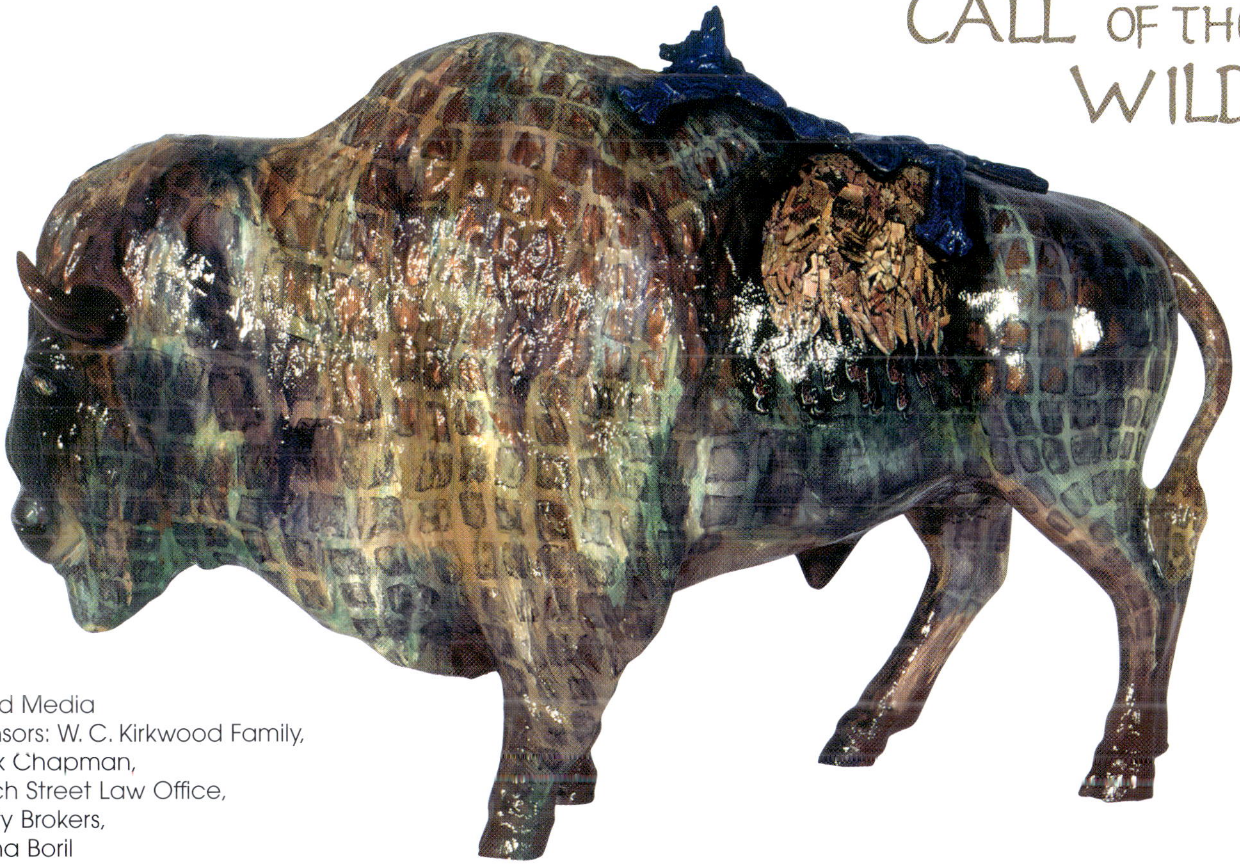

Mixed Media
Sponsors: W. C. Kirkwood Family,
Frank Chapman,
Beech Street Law Office,
Equity Brokers,
Ronna Boril

" 'The Buffalo is gone,' Francis Parkman, historian of the west wrote in 1892, '...wolves have succumbed to arsenic and hushed their savage music.... The mountain lion shrinks from the face of man and even Old Ephraim, the grizzly bear, seeks the seclusion of his dens and caverns.' It is this history of endangerment that led me to create my Buffalo as a satirical portrait which pays tribute to the endangered species of the world.
"My grandmother introduced me to the joys of art museums and creating art at an early age and as an artist and designer I still practice that experimental and playful approach."

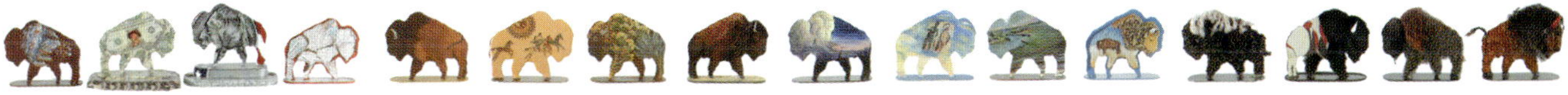

Charles Parson

B.T. (BUFFALO TERRAIN)

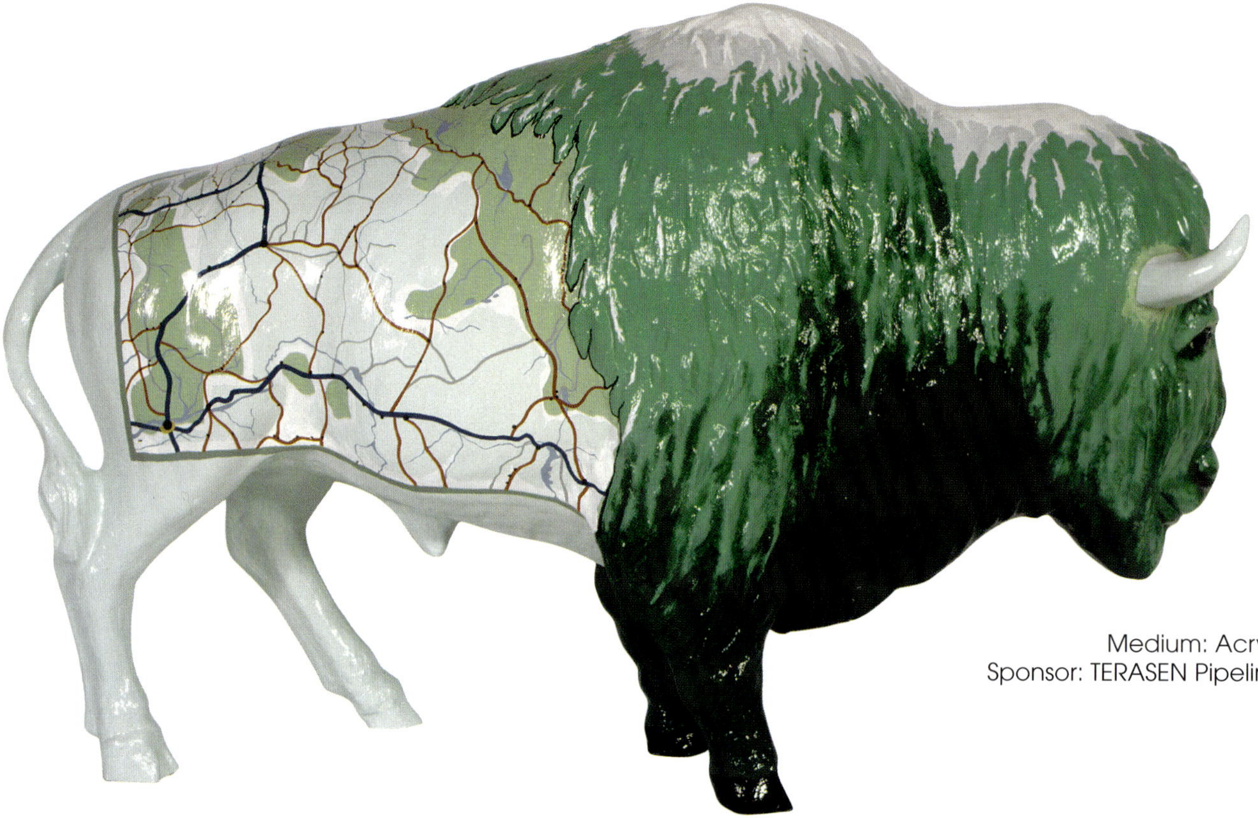

Medium: Acrylic
Sponsor: TERASEN Pipelines

"Inspiration came from my travels throughout Wyoming, combined with my work of looking at same places, during different times. I work as a contract muralist for Denver Museum of Nature and Science, while also exhibiting large scale abstract sculptures. I presented a full-gallery installation at the Nic in 1999, *A Sense of Place*. My book, *A Sense of Place* is available in the NIC bookstore."

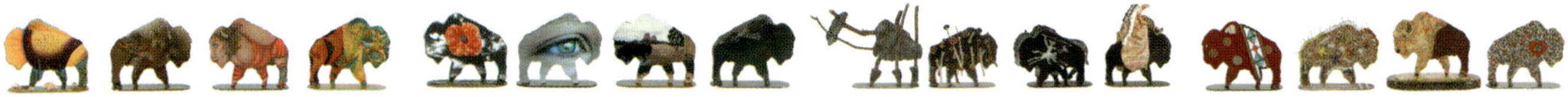

Arin Waddell

BUFFALO GRASS

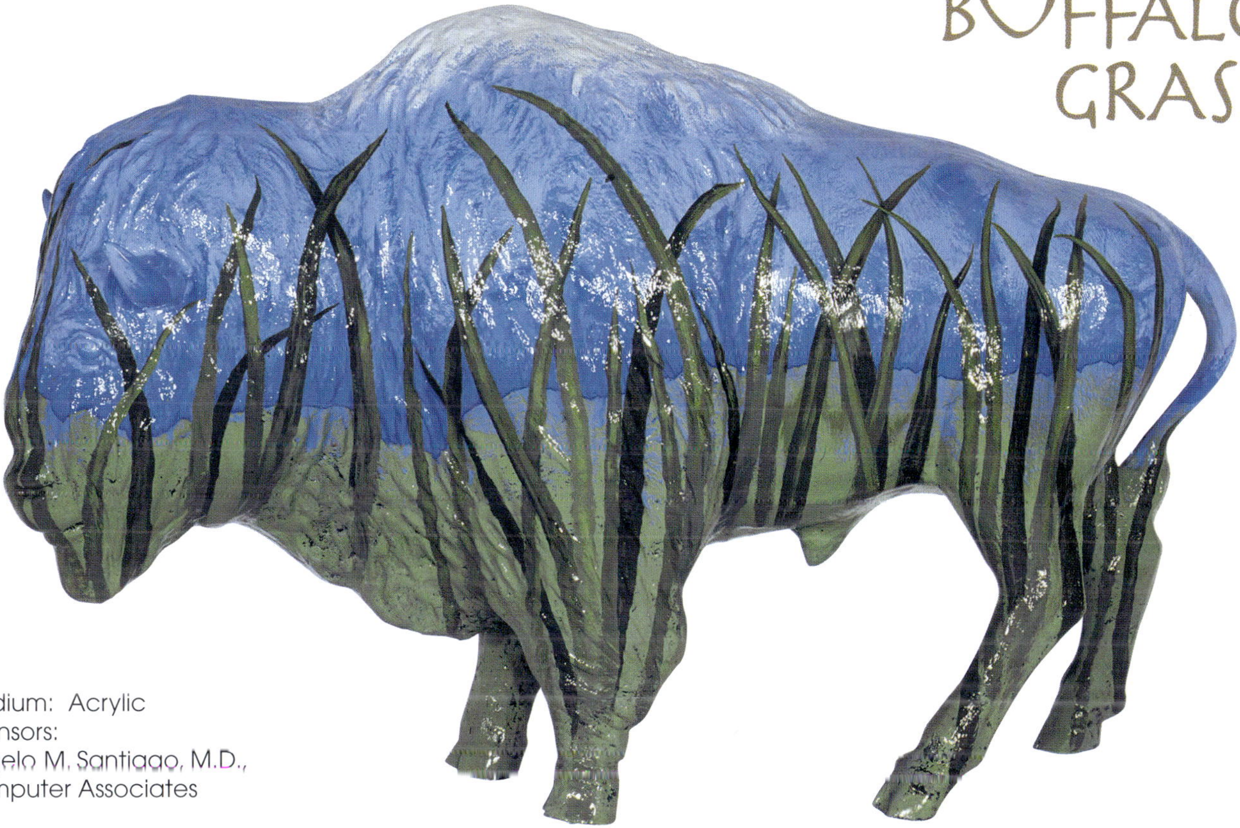

Medium: Acrylic
Sponsors:
Angelo M. Santiago, M.D.,
Computer Associates

"I adore visual and verbal puns. I roll words and images around, or work them like odd puzzle pieces until I find something that clicks. After that, it's a matter of technical/visual problem-solving.

"I have faith as an artist; if I can make art with two tiny children and a work-a-holic husband, anyone can do it. My studio is a zoo, of late, and a sanctuary."

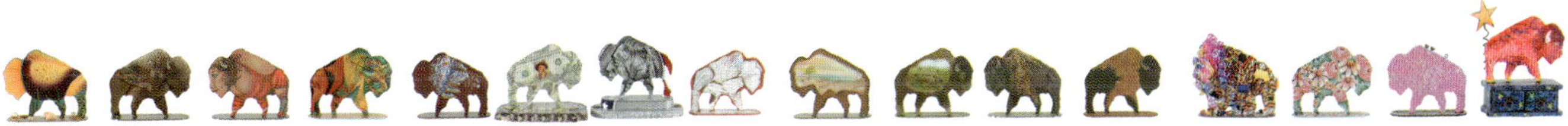

Deb Penk

ROAMING FREE

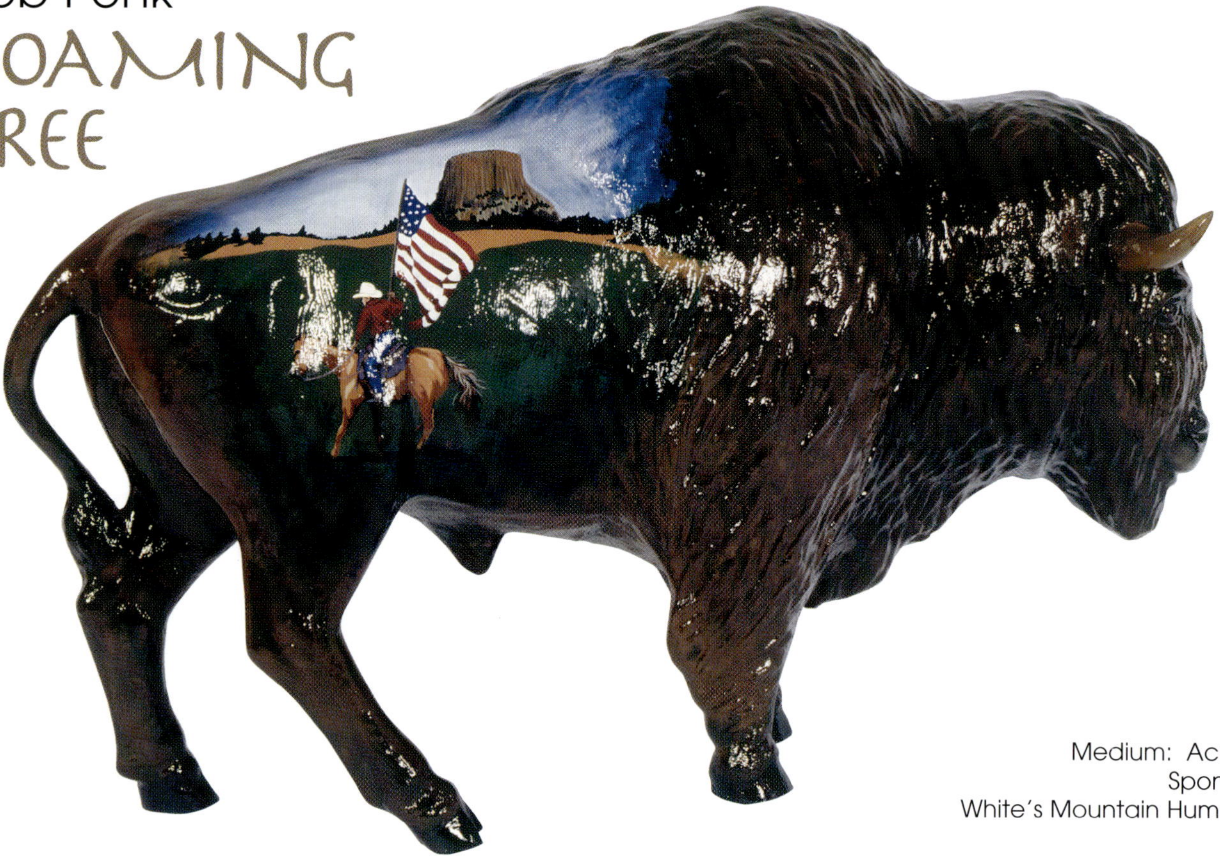

Medium: Acrylic
Sponsor:
White's Mountain Hummer

"Bill (I called him Bill, because he made a *statement*!), was a wonderful guest for me. He was instantly my friend! His presence made me feel as I do when viewing them in Yellowstone, free, roaming. Recently completing my wish of visiting all 50 states, I am still proud to be a Wyomingite. Like Bill here, I plan on being free to roam Wyoming for a very long time.

"Second Chapter of 'Bill:' I felt sad to give Bill up. He became a part of my lifestyle. The good news is that a real Buffalo has made himself a home around my house in Jackson. He appeared almost the same time as Bill left. This Buffalo is roaming around the neighborhood, doing as he will. The first day he stood between my mailbox and my car, I decided to name him 'Bill.' too."

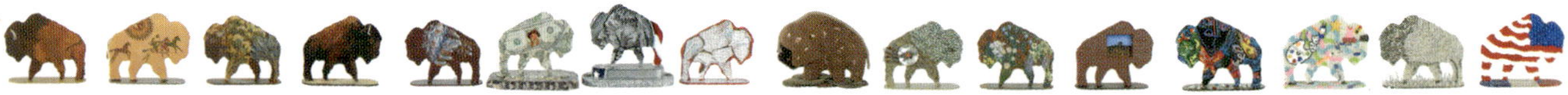

Lynn Newman
IN A DREAM

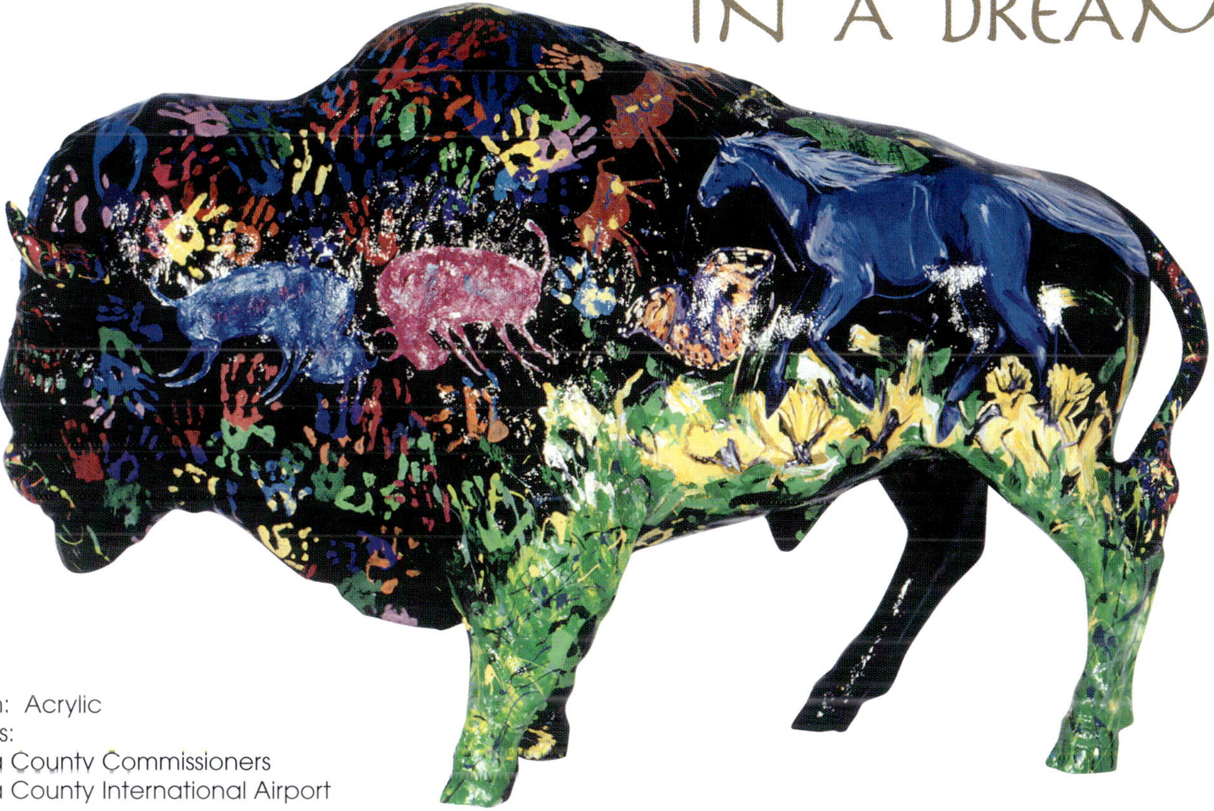

Medium: Acrylic
Sponsors:
Natrona County Commissioners
Natrona County International Airport

"The inspiration for this Buffalo was based on poetry, children and Native American art which open the windows to new worlds. I'm very pleased that I'll be able to make connections with my family and home state when North Dakota State University in Fargo sponsors an exhibit of my work this October."

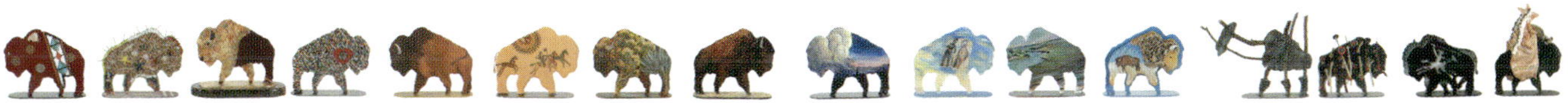

Steve Schrepferman

BUFFALOED BUFFALO

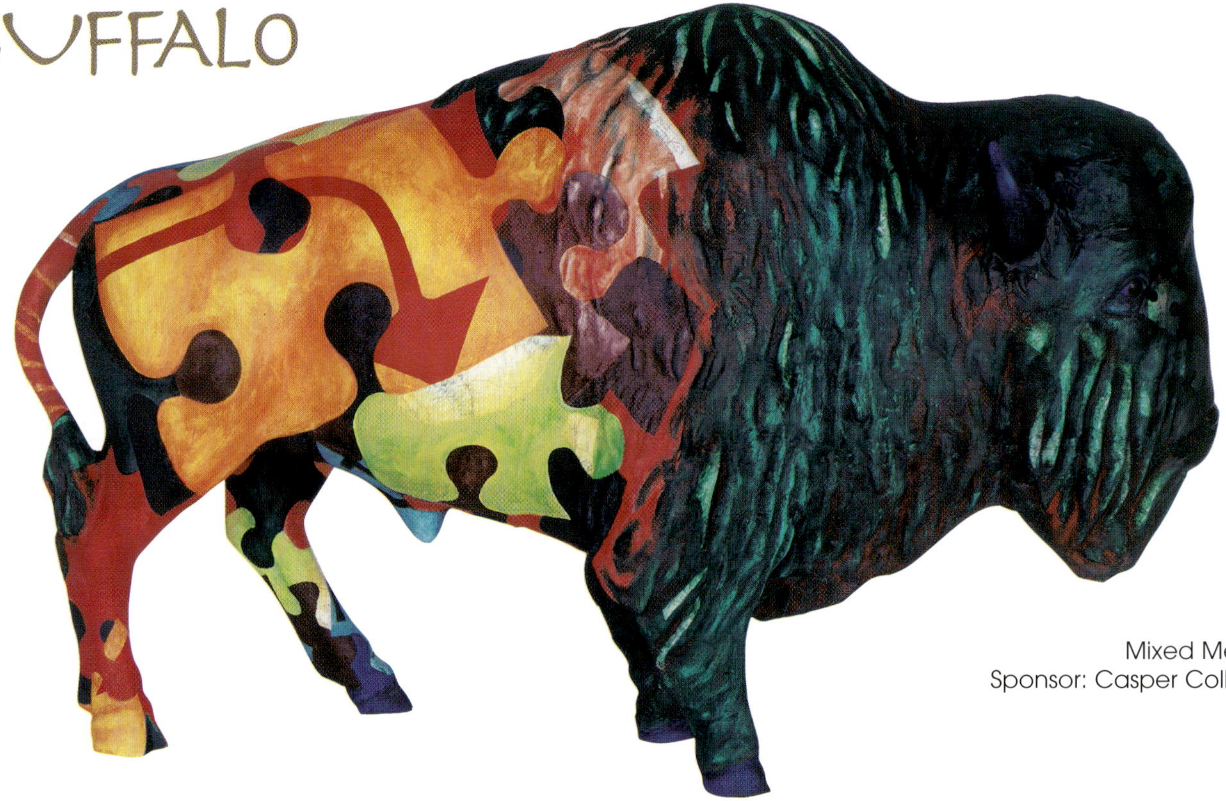

Mixed Media
Sponsor: Casper College

"The term 'being buffaloed'— confused, fooled, mixed up — offered a wide variety of visual ideas to play with on this bison.
"I am a clay artist who leans toward abstracted ideas. I love word play, working visual ideas with concepts."

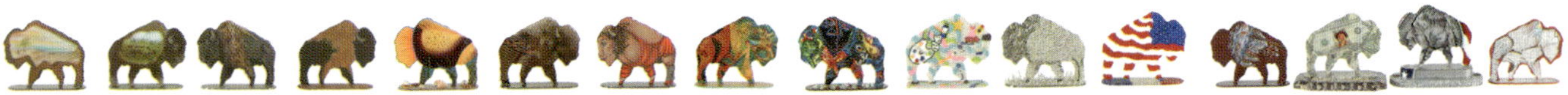

Michele McDonald

SUNDOWNER

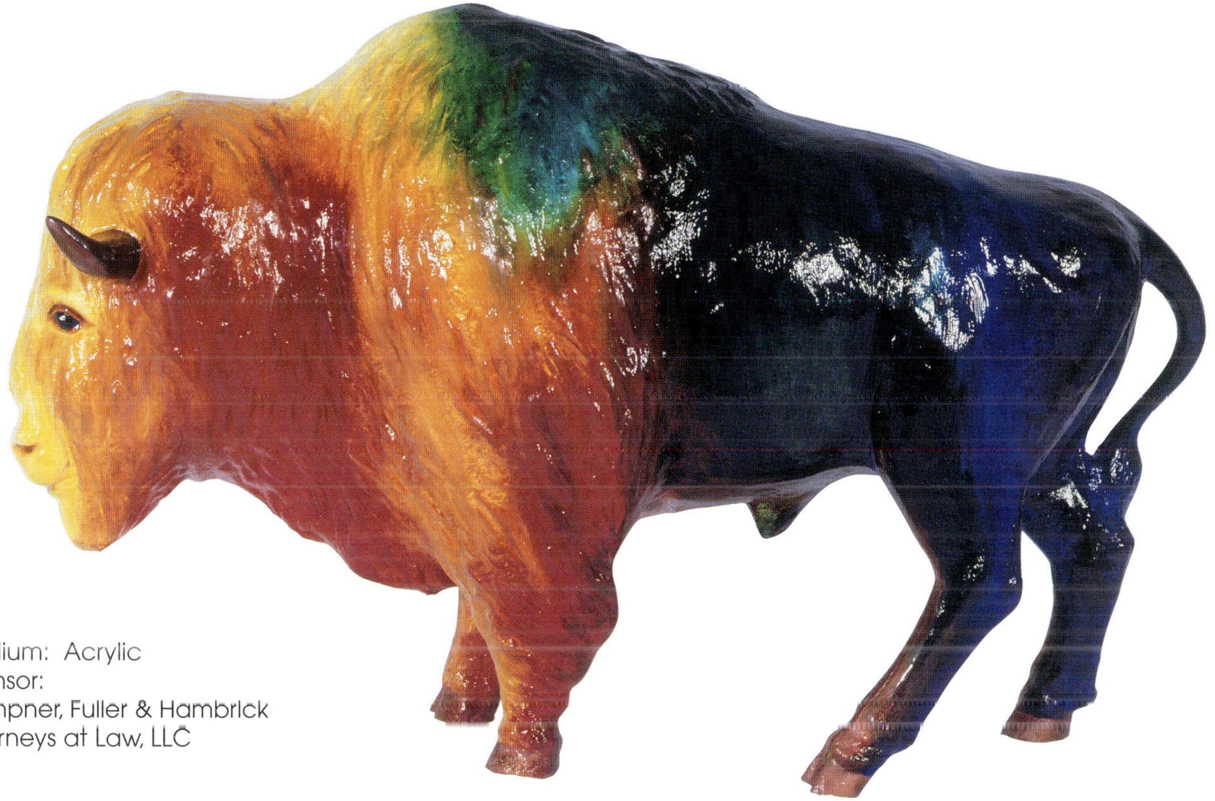

Medium: Acrylic
Sponsor:
Krampner, Fuller & Hambrick
Attorneys at Law, LLC

"I envisioned my Buffalo walking into a sunset. Sunlit colors on his face and shoulders turning into midnight colors toward the back."

Michele is a Wyoming native who teaches watercolor & mixed media classes at the Casper Recreation Center. She is also a professional artist who creates watercolor and acrylic paintings with the luminosity of stained glass. Michele is a signature member of the National Acrylic Painters Association and the Northwest Watercolor Society.

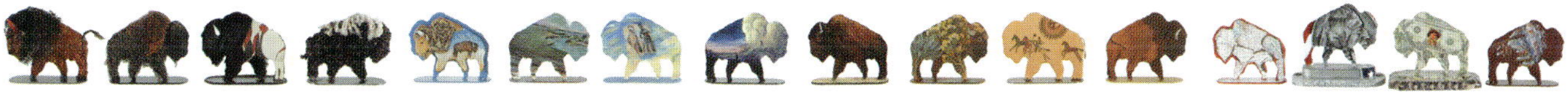

Laura Tegenu

KNIGHT ON THE TOWN

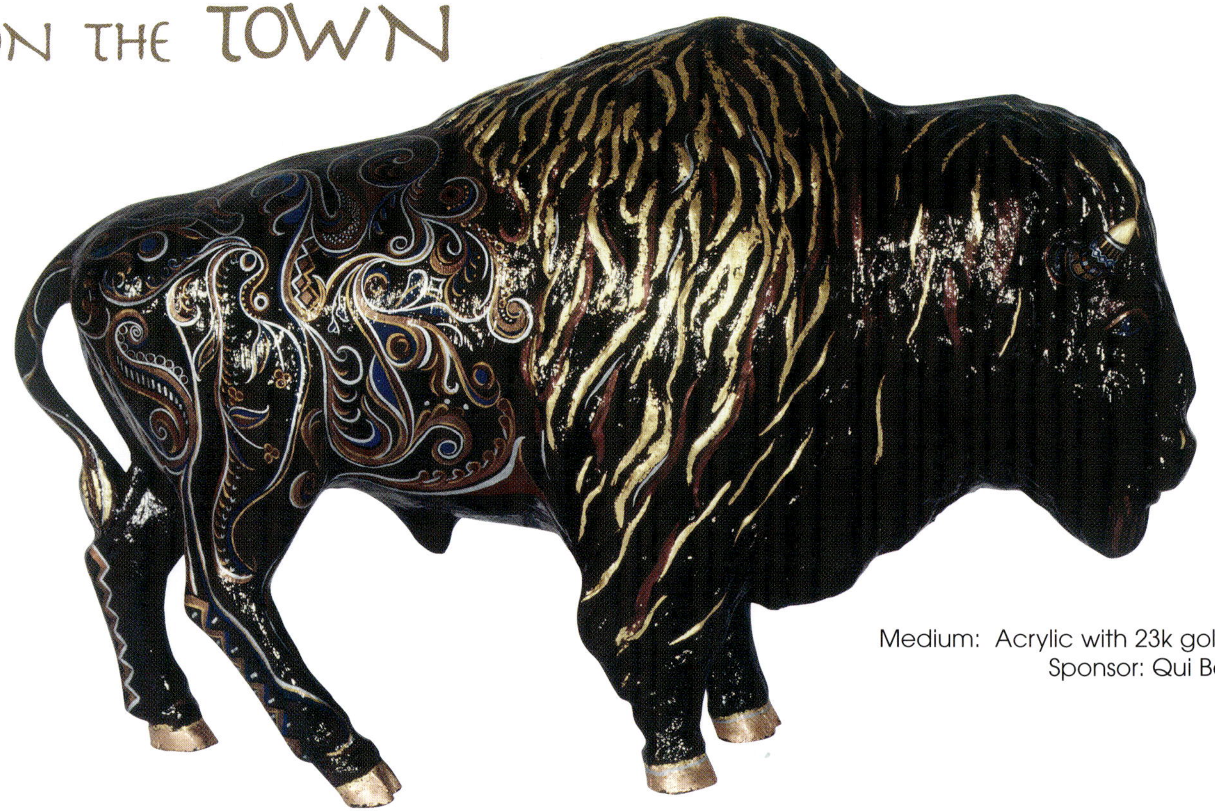

Medium: Acrylic with 23k gold leaf
Sponsor: Qui Bee Art

"The Buffalo has such a dramatic presence, I felt he should be clothed in the richest finery for an evening on the town."
Laura Tegenu has been a muralist in the Casper area since 1991. Her business name is *Walls and All.*

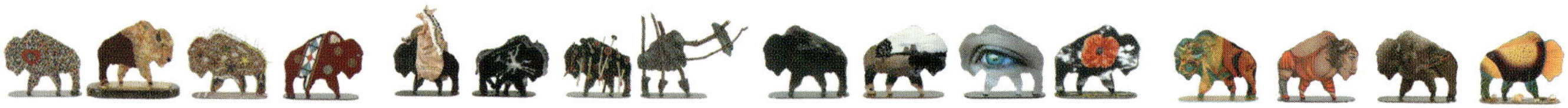

Jim Kopp
PROGRESS

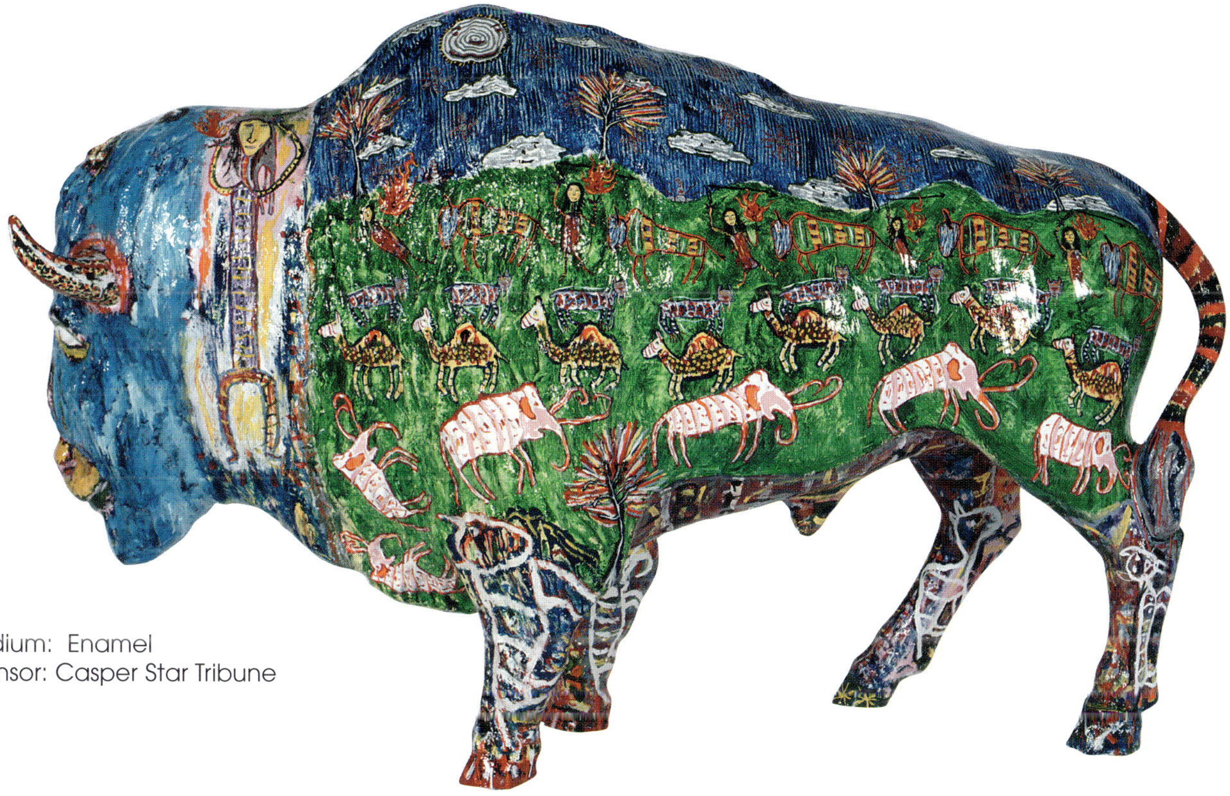

Medium: Enamel
Sponsor: Casper Star Tribune

"Since the Buffalo has survived through many horrendous conditions for such a long time, the idea of its history was my main source of inspiration.
"I am a self-taught artist who has no formal training and I rely on imagination rather than technique, and energy rather than rhetoric."

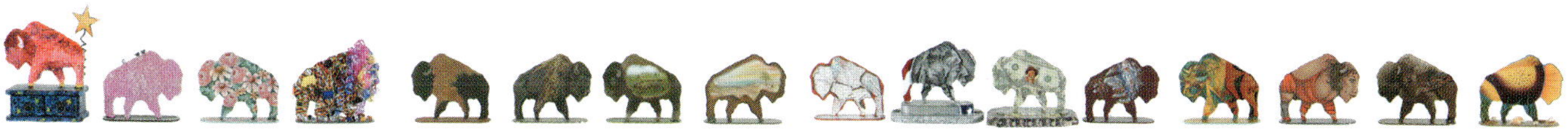

ACKNOWLEDGEMENTS

Artist Committee:
Holly Turner, Barbara Kuxhausen, Jessica Jones, Toni Garrard & Carol Plummer

Logistics Committee:
John Lowe, Gary Berchenbriter, Jessica Jones & Holly Turner

Marketing Committee:
Margaret Benson, Nadia White & Holly Turner

Merchandise Committee:
Holly Turner, Sidney Thompson, Kelly Beurskens, TimAnn Day & Nancy Witzeling

Food Committee: Betsy Dowell

Sponsor Committee: Kate Tiernan & Holly Turner

Photography: Bruce Nichols, Mountain Sun Photo

Copywriting: Kate Tiernan & Charlotte Babcock

Auctioneers: Annie & Amy Smith

Auction Committee:
Julie Sexton, Helen Brown, Jodi Foss, Jeanne Goldrick & Holly Turner

Casper Public Service Director & Transportation Guru: Philip Stuckert

City of Casper Zoning Tsar: Doug Lake

Armors • Casper Concrete • Casper Cake & Donut
City of Casper • Coliseum Motor Co. • Fiberstock • House of Printing
Kistler Tent & Awning Co • Merback Award Co.

The NIC Board
Gary Berchenbriter (Chair), Margaret Benson, Steve Emery, John Lowe,
Sandi Matthews, Bill Mixer (Vice Chair), Sidney Thompson, Lynne Whalen,
Nadia White, Fritzi Wilson (Secretary), Tom Loepp, Rachel Chadderdon & Echo Bale

The NIC Staff
Holly Turner, Kate Tiernan, Patricia Ruppert, Toni Garrard, Jessica Jones,
Kelly Beurskens, TimAnn Day, Stuart Crowder, Dandee Pattee, Tess Tubbs,
Robert White & Don Poste

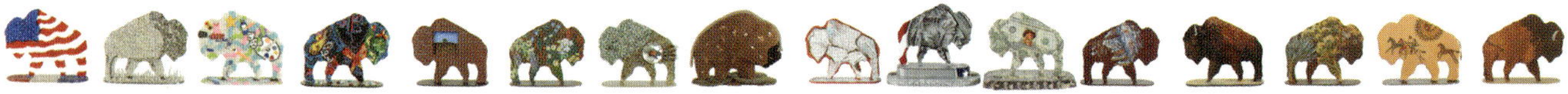

ARTIST INFORMATION

Additional information on the aritists is available online at: wherethebuffaloroam.org

Joe Arnold • Laramie, WY
YELLOWSTONE BUFFALO
307-745-6214
artist82070@yahoo.com

Ginny Butcher • Evansville, WY
O, GIVE ME A HOME
307-377-6163

Jen Champlin • Powell, WY
SHARDS IN SAND
307-754-6212

Annette Chaudet
Greybull, WY
BUFFALO ROBE
pronghornpress.org

Dennis Cumin • Billings, MT
BLUFFING BUFFALO
406-252-5877

B.J. Durr • Wheatland, WY
TRIBUTE TO THE BUFFALO
307-322-2117

John Giarrizzo • Powell, WY
DISTANT THUNDER
(IN RED AND BLACK)

Debra Hall & Patti Ginglos
Casper, WY
LEWIS & CLARK
ANNIVERSARY RENDITION

Sonja Huff, Nancy Stroh,
Karen Henneck • Casper, WY
ART HISTORY 101
307-265-9508

Jim Kopp • Casper, WY
PROGRESS
307.235.4670
jim@jimkopp.com

Linda Lillegraven
Laramie, WY
EMERGING FROM
THE PLEISTOCENE

Tom Loepp
Casper, WY
NICALO
307-472-4225

Michele McDonald
Casper, WY
SUNDOWNER
307-265-1518
studiomichele@coffey.com

Sharon Merschat
Casper, WY
CALL OF THE WILD
307-265-6942
sharonm@trib.com

Chris Navarro • Casper, WY
BUFFALO SPIRIT
307-234-5547

Lynn Newman
Cheyenne, WY
IN A DREAM
307-771-2663
newm773@aol.com

Charles Parson
Lakewood, CO
B.T. (BUFFALO TERRAIN)
303-238-2706

Deb Penk • Casper, WY
ROAMING FREE
Dietrapenk@aol.com

Linda Raynolds
Cody, WY
MOTHER OF MILLIONS
307-587-3694
lsr00@tritel.net

Kevin Red Star
& Sunny Sky
Roberts, MT
PROVIDER OF THE
PLAINS INDIANS
www.kevinredstar.com

Edie Reno • Gilette, WY
WYOMING SONGS
307-686-4713

Linda L. Ryan • Casper, WY
WHITE BUFFALO
307-237-4776

Steve Schrepferman
Cody, WY
THE BUFFALOED BUFFALO
307-587-6693
schrepferman@vcn.com

Robert Seabeck
Laramie, WY
BIG MIKE
307-742-7956

Laura Tegenu • Casper, WY
KNIGHT ON THE TOWN
307-237-5303

Lynn Thorpe • Powell, WY
SYNONYMOUS
307-754-2856
thorpel@vcn.com

Arin Waddell • Dayton, WY
BUFFALO GRASS
307-655-3147
awaddell@fiberpipe.net

Theodore Waddell
Manhattan, MT
POLLOCK'S BUFFALO
(ID): 208-788-4953
(MT): 408-284-6803

The Wyoming Watercolor
Company:
Holly Bishop,
Jim Gaither,
Skip Larcom,
Barbara Kuxhausen,
Michele McDonald,
& Joan Melius
Casper, WY
THE LUV BUFF

Kathryn Yauney
Rawlins, WY
BUFFALO PEOPLE
307-324-6902

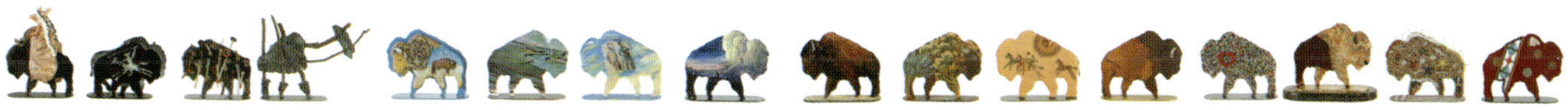

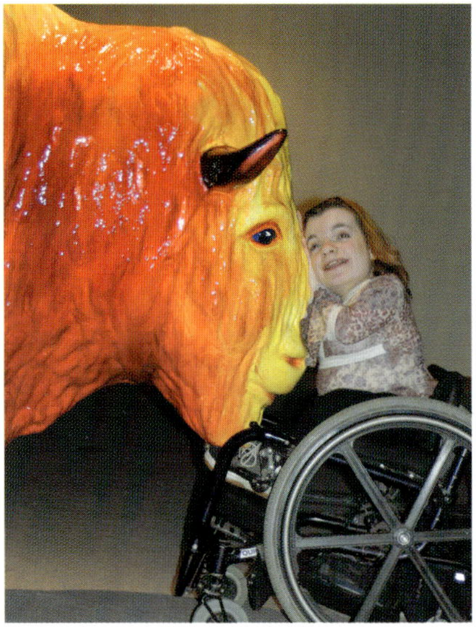

P.S.

If you want to know
more about the
Nicolaysen Art Museum
please write us at:

400 E Collins,
Casper WY 82601

or call

307-235-5247

or find us on the web at

thenic.org

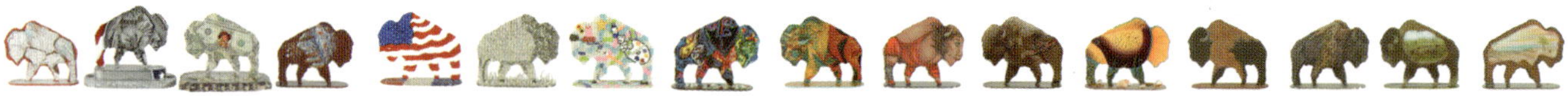